FRENCHTOWN CEMETERY

OLD CATHOLIC BURYING GROUND

PRAIRIE DU CHIEN, WISCONSIN • 1816-1840

HISTORY AND BURIALS

MARY ELISE ANTOINE

LITTLE CREEK PRESS®
AND BOOK DESIGN
MINERAL POINT, WISCONSIN

Little Creek Press.
5341 Sunny Ridge Road
Mineral Point, WI 53565

ORDERING INFORMATION
Quantity sales. Special discounts are available on quantity purchases by corporations, associations, and others. For details, contact info@littlecreekpress.com

Orders by US trade bookstores and wholesalers.
Please contact Little Creek Press or Ingram for details.

Printed in the United States of America

Cataloging-in-Publication Data
Names: Antoine, Mary Elise, author.
Title: Frenchtown Cemetery, Old Catholic Burying Ground, Prairie du Chien, Wisconsin, 1816-1840, History and Burials / Mary Elise Antoine
Description: Mineral Point, WI: Little Creek Press, 2022.
Identifiers: LCCN: 2022912863 | ISBN: 978-1-955656-29-0
Subjects: BIOGRAPHY & AUTOBIOGRAPHY / Culture, Ethnic & Regional

Book design by Little Creek Press

Cover Image: Rev. A. Philip Kremer offers Mass at the Old Catholic Burying Ground, circa 1890-1900. (Private Collection)

Dedicated to...

Jim. Thank you for all the conversations we had about the early French residents of Prairie du Chien. These visits made the trips to Madison for staff meetings worthwhile.

Acknowledgments

Thank you to Kristin, Peggy, and the staff of Little Creek Press. Your kindness and skills made this work a reality.

Contents

Introduction

Located north of the city limits of Prairie du Chien lies a small cemetery. It is situated on the west side of County Highway K, which the life-long residents of Prairie du Chien still call "Frenchtown Road." An old, welded wire fence defines the boundaries of this small burying ground. Rough weather-beaten stones, seemingly scattered about, mark gentle grass-covered depressions. Two crypts of hewn limestone and the remains of two other crypts stand against the west fence line. To the right, two broken head stones crookedly mark the last burials in the cemetery.

Frenchtown Road was the northern part of a path that had been marked on an early 19th century map as "Highway." The oldest thoroughfare on the prairie, this dirt path followed the contours of the east bank of the Mississippi River but was set back upon somewhat higher land so that the road remained passable when the waters of the river rose each spring.

In 1820, Isaac Lee, from the Surveyor General's Office in Detroit, drew a rough map of the prairie delineating the location of plats of land claimed by the residents of Prairie du Chien. On the map, Lee called the trail the "Highway." This highway stretched over twelve miles from the marshy ground of the Wisconsin River to pass slightly east of the Old French Fort and along the west boundaries of the farm lots and then passing the Old Catholic Burying Ground as it wound northward to end at Rolette's Mill. By 1820, the northern half of the highway connected two villages: the Village of St. Friole and the Upper Village. The Old Catholic Burying Ground stood between the two villages. A large island across the *marais* from the Village of St. Friole was the Main Village.[1]

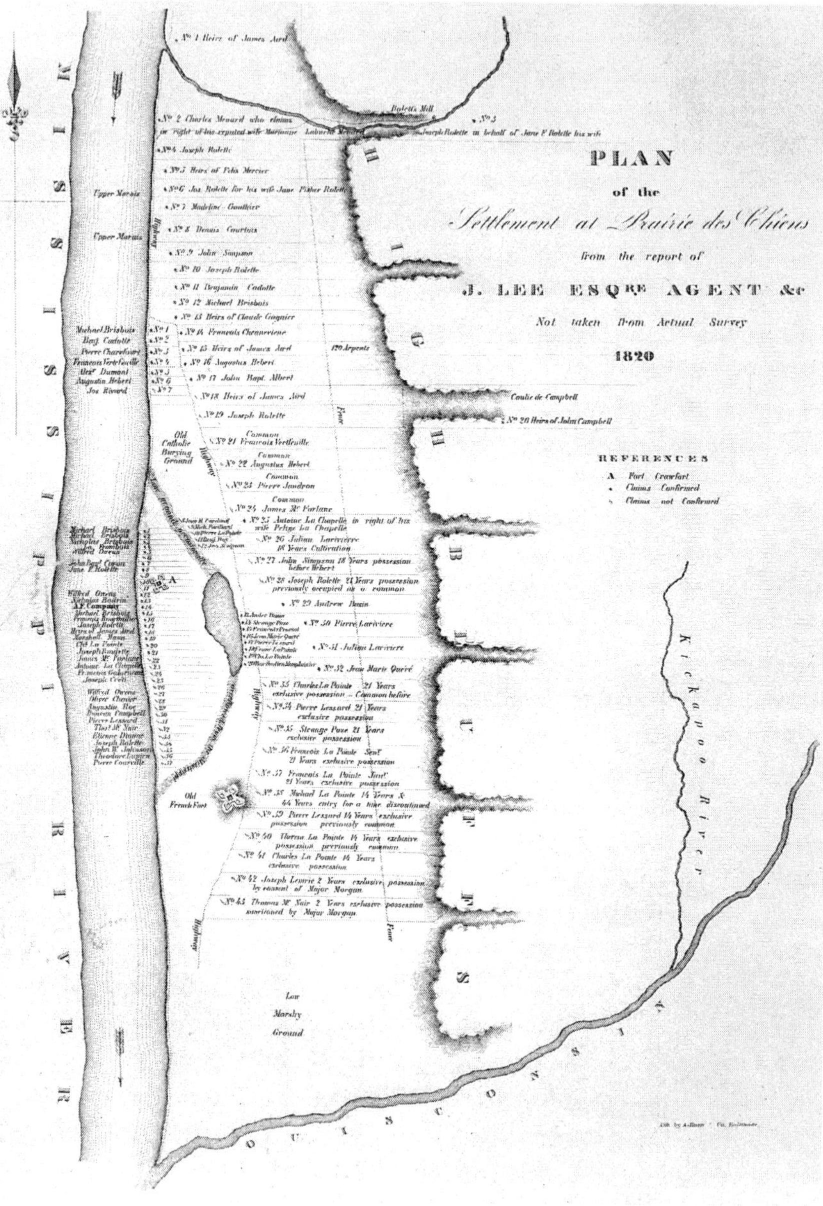

Plan of the Settlement at Prairie des Chiens from the report of I. Lee Esqre. Agent &c. 1820. The earliest map and image of Prairie du Chien detailed the location of the Old Catholic Burying Ground. (Private Collection)

In 1872, the City of Prairie du Chien was incorporated. The Main Village and the Village of St. Friole lost their independent designation and were now part of the city. The section of the "Highway" within the city limits was named Main Street. The northern section of the "Highway," beyond the city limits, remained a dirt path. Wide enough to accommodate a wagon pulled by a team of horses, the path connected the City of Prairie du Chien to the small community on the north end of the prairie that Lee had named the Upper Village. As most of the residents of the old Upper Village were the descendants of the early French-Canadian settlers of Prairie du Chien, the roadway came to be called Frenchtown Road. Along Frenchtown Road stood the log homes of families with last names recalling the days of the voyageurs: Pion, Chenevert, Vertefeuille, Caya, Cherrier, Lessard, Gardepie. The road turned eastward at a backwater of the Mississippi River named Courtois Lake and then turned northeast to end at Rolette's mill. When the land fronting the lake passed to Denis Courtois' daughter and son-in-law, the name changed to Grimard Lake. In time, Grimard was Angelized to Gremore, and the site of Rolette's mill became Mill Coulee.

Like the road and the lake, the small cemetery has been given many names. In the first half of the 19th century, it was the Old Catholic Burying Ground. As more people of different nationalities moved to Prairie du Chien, the cemetery was looked upon as culturally distinct and called the old French Cemetery or the Frenchtown Cemetery. In the 20th century, local historians addressed the cemetery in the way they thought the early residents of the community might have referred to it. A plaque listing the people thought to be buried in the cemetery was erected within the confines of the grounds, and they titled the cemetery *l'ancien Cimetiere Français*.

The lack of constancy in a name for the cemetery reflects the fragile status of the burying ground from its very beginning. The first burying ground for the residents of Prairie du Chien had been sited on the Main Village island. With the arrival of the United States Army on the prairie in 1816, the residents of Prairie du Chien were ordered to select a new location for their burying ground.[2] They chose a site far from the authoritarian presence of the military and hopefully therefore safe.

The new cemetery site shows that careful consideration went into the choice for the location of the burying ground for all the residents of the prairie. The new cemetery would be on high ground above the threat of flooding, and it was centrally located. By 1816, the three villages existed on the prairie. The new cemetery was just off the dirt path that connected the Upper Village to the Village of St. Friole and across the *marais* (slough) from the Main Village.

In 1817, Father Marie Joseph Dunand arrived at the prairie. He was the first Catholic priest to visit Prairie du Chien and on May 10 blessed "the parish cemetery." In the short time he was on the prairie, he officiated at one burial, but it was the responsibility of the residents to maintain the records of all future burials until the arrival of another priest.[3] Father François Vincent Badin arrived at Prairie du Chien in June 1827, ten years after Father Dunand. Father Badin maintained a record of the burials he blessed.[4] But, from the end of his last visit in 1829 until Father Augustin Ravoux came to Prairie du Chien in 1840, there is no indication that anyone, religious or secular, kept a record of burials that occurred in Prairie du Chien. While Catholic priests visited to minister to the needs of the residents, and Father Samuel Mazzuchelli began the construction of St. Gabriel's Church, there was no permanent priest in residence on the prairie until 1840. In that year, Bishop Mathias Loras sent Father Augustin Ravoux to Prairie du Chien to be the pastor of St. Gabriel's Parish. He established a register for the parish in which he recorded baptisms, marriages, and burials. He also laid out a new cemetery behind St. Gabriel's Church. From that date onward, the priests assumed that the Catholic residents of the prairie, upon their death, would be interred in St. Gabriel's Cemetery. Each burial was carefully recorded in the register.[5]

In 1836, Strange Powers had given the land on which St. Gabriel's Church and its cemetery would be established to Bishop Frederic Rese of the newly established Diocese of Detroit and the representative of the Catholic Church.[6] That same month, Hercules L. Dousman also gave a tract of land to Bishop Rese "for the specific use of a burying ground." Half of the land would be a "Public Burying Ground," and the western portion was to be a Catholic burying ground.[7] This tract of land given by Dousman was located along the "Highway" directly east of the Old Catholic Burying Ground.

With two new cemeteries, the Old Catholic Burying Ground fell into disuse. It was not maintained by St. Gabriel's Parish nor by any arm of the Catholic Church. Fences, headstones, and burial markers deteriorated. Grass, weeds, and small trees grew in abandon. The fences that had once been erected to mark a burial rotted and disappeared. The burying ground was never forgotten, though. For a few years, the pastor of St. Gabriel's parish offered an annual Mass at the cemetery.

In the early 20th century, people began to show an interest in the cemetery. Individuals whose ancestors were buried in the cemetery cut

In the late 1800s, the pastor of St. Gabriel's parish celebrated the Mass at the Old Catholic burying grounds. (Prairie du Chien Historical Society)

grass, cleared trees, and attempted to mark burial sites. Women who were members of the St. Vincent de Paul Sewing Society placed the wire fence around the visible remains of the cemetery and painted the fence and cross of the Gardepie grave. They had wished to do more, but by then it was hard to determine who was buried in the cemetery and where each grave was located.[8]

Old Catholic Burying Ground or Frenchtown Cemetery as it looked circa 1900. (Private Collection)

At mid-century, the Prairie du Chien Women's Civic Club and then, about the same time, the State Historical Society of Wisconsin erected signs in the midst of the burials. Since then, interest in the cemetery has grown. Today, the Township of Prairie du Chien maintains the burial grounds. Descendants of the early French-Canadian residents of Prairie du Chien return to the prairie looking for a connection to their ancestors. And that connection is often found in the "old French Cemetery."

Green Bay, Prairie du Chien, and La Pointe on Madeline Island are the earliest places of permanent European settlement in Wisconsin. All three were established and settled by French-speaking people. Like Prairie du Chien, the other two communities had burying grounds for

The Old Catholic Burying Ground with markers expressing the various names the burying ground has been given, circa 1967. (Prairie du Chien Historical Society)

its first residents; but for different reasons neither of those cemeteries has survived.

At Green Bay, from 1745 until 1835, people of all faiths were buried in La Baye Burial Place near the house of Pierre Grignon. In 1835, the area around the early settlement of La Baye (Green Bay) was expanding. One of the new communities formed along the Fox River was Astor. The site chosen for this planned community included the La Baye Burial Place. The developers decided that the graves therefore needed to be relocated. Most of the markers on the graves in this cemetery had ceased to exist by 1835, making identification of the graves difficult. Descendants of the people buried in the cemetery were asked to identify which graves were Catholic and which were not. Catholic remains were placed in a mass grave in the cemetery east of St. John the Evangelist Church. Non-Catholic remains were placed in two locations: Whitney Park and Baird Place. The remains buried in Baird Place were relocated once again after the Civil War and now are in Woodlawn Cemetery.[9]

As there was a fort and a Catholic mission established at La Pointe under the French regime, it is assumed that people had died and were buried on Madeline Island. If there were early burials, the location or locations are not known. When Father Frederic Baraga came to the island in 1835, he established St. Joseph's Mission, constructed a church, and in 1836 consecrated the cemetery associated with the mission. This cemetery may have been the site of an earlier burial ground, but burial records for La Pointe begin with Father Baraga.[10]

Though left to nature for many years, the Old Catholic Burying Ground at Prairie du Chien did not suffer the fate of the early cemeteries of Green Bay and La Pointe. A sense of honor and sanctity of the burials in the Old Catholic Burying Ground persisted. The men, women, and children who had been buried in the cemetery were not reinterred in the newer cemeteries. The burying ground and its people were acknowledged.

Few of the early French-Canadian residents at Prairie du Chien could read or write. These fur traders, voyageurs, and their families may have told stories of their lives, their journeys, and their hardships. If so, few stories were recorded for future generations. But I believe the history of the Old Catholic Burying Ground at Prairie du Chien and the men, women, and children buried there provide an opportunity for learning about them and about early 19th century *la Prairie des Chiens*.

As I began to research the history of the old cemetery, I came to realize that the existence of the cemetery was a direct result of occurrences far greater than the events of daily life at Prairie du Chien. Why the cemetery came into existence can be seen as a consequence of the United States national policy after the War of 1812 to gain political control of the western reaches of the Northwest Territory. This frontier policy continued along the upper Mississippi until the territories of Iowa, Wisconsin, and Minnesota were established. This period of change in the upper Mississippi River valley—1816 through 1840—is the era which brackets the years in which the cemetery was the only burial ground for the residents of Prairie du Chien.

At the same time as the United States was pushing its political agenda westward, Christian faiths competed with one another in attempts to "Christianize" the thousands of Indigenous people who lived in the Northwest Territory. The Catholic priests who had left

Europe to be missionaries in the new United States territories were the first to appreciate the spiritual needs of the families living in the isolated French communities with roots in the French Regime that were part of the Northwest Territory. Father Marie Joseph Dunand was the first of many missionaries to bring spiritual contact to Prairie du Chien. Other Catholic priests and Protestant ministers followed Dunand's practice up until 1836—the same year the United States Congress established the Territory of Wisconsin—by which time two other cemeteries and three churches had been established at Prairie du Chien. The history of the Old Catholic Burying Ground at Prairie du Chien is part of the history of Wisconsin and the United States.

While the history of the Old Catholic Burying Ground is an important part of the history of early Prairie du Chien and the Wisconsin territory, any discussion of the cemetery poses an important question: "Who is buried in the 'old French Cemetery'?" The State Historical Society of Wisconsin dedicated a metal marker for the cemetery in 1967. On it, the Society listed the names of people believed to be buried on the grounds. Several websites contain the same listing of names. But, I wondered, are these lists correct? So, I set about the task of determining just who is buried in the cemetery. As is often the case, the answer to this question is not simple.

First, I examined the records maintained by the Catholic priests who ministered to the residents of Prairie du Chien from 1817 through 1870. These records include the register of Father Marie Joseph Dunand, which is held by the Catholic Diocese of La Crosse. The record is written in French. It has been translated and published by James L. Hansen. The records of Father François Vincent Badin are held by the archives of St. Mary's College in Montreal, Canada. A photostatic copy is owned by the Wisconsin Historical Society. Father Badin also wrote in French, and James Hansen translated the record into English. I also read through the correspondence and notes of Father Samuel Mazzuchelli, records maintained by Bishop Mathias Loras, and the register begun by Father Augustin Ravoux in 1840 and continued by his successors at St.

Gabriel's Parish. All these documents contain information on baptisms, confirmations, marriages, and burials. Based upon these records, a list of documented burials was compiled.

There are many gaps in the records maintained from 1817 until 1840, because there were periods in which no priest was at Prairie du Chien. For instance, ten years passed from the time Father Dunand left Prairie du Chien until Father Badin arrived in the spring of 1827. After Father Badin left the upper Mississippi in 1829, other missionary priests visited Prairie du Chien, including Samuel Mazzuchelli. But all the priests' visits were short in duration and sporadic. It can be assumed that some people living on the prairie may have died while a priest was present as well as during the periods in which no priest ministered to the Catholics of Prairie du Chien. The deceased therefore surely were buried in the cemetery, as this was the only burying ground for the community until 1840.

I therefore researched the records maintained by the Register in Probate for Crawford County from 1818 to 1854. Not surprisingly, I discovered that many people residing at Prairie du Chien died during this time. The estates of the deceased were probated. Included in the probate documents were the estates of the French-speaking men whose burials had been recorded in the registers maintained by the Catholic priests. But the probate records also documented the deaths of other men and a few women. Their deaths had occurred during the times when no priest resided at Prairie du Chien. Almost all of the men and the women were of French-Canadian Catholic ancestry. So, I now had the beginning of a list of people probably buried in the Old Catholic Burying Ground, in addition to those people for which a burial had been recorded.

But with a lack of burial records, another question arose based upon the documents filed with the Register in Probate. Had all the men whose estates had been probated in Crawford County died at Prairie du Chien? More research was needed.

In the early 19th century, Prairie du Chien was part of Indiana Territory and then Illinois Territory and was under the jurisdiction of St. Clair County. When Illinois was admitted to the Union in 1818, the northern portion of what had been Illinois Territory came under the jurisdiction of Michigan Territory. In 1818, two counties were established for the western section of Michigan Territory. Brown County included all the land north of the State of Illinois from Lake Michigan to a north-south line drawn along the southerly flow of the Wisconsin River. Crawford County comprised all the land north of Illinois and west from the north-south line to the Mississippi River. As the only settlement in Crawford County, Prairie du Chien was made the county seat. So, if someone died, and he or she had property anywhere in the vast expanse of Crawford County, the estate was probated at Prairie du Chien. However, just because the estate was probated at Prairie du Chien did not mean the person died at Prairie du Chien and was buried at Prairie du Chien. Examples of people who died while not in Prairie du Chien at the time of their deaths are Pierre Paquette, Antoine Brisbois, François Bouthillier, Edward Pizanne, and Pierre Dispouts. All these men owned property in Prairie du Chien, and their estates were probated in Crawford County; but records prove that none of the men were buried on the prairie.

Most of the people, though, whose estates were probated at Prairie du Chien during this time period were buried at Prairie du Chien. Some estate records include bills for digging a grave or making a coffin. The Old Catholic Burying Ground was the only cemetery for the community until 1840 and the beginning of the *registre* created by Father Ravoux; so it can be assumed that the men and women living at Prairie du Chien who died prior to 1840 were interred in this burial ground. For the men who died in 1836 and the years after, I checked to see if they had been buried in either of the two new cemeteries, St. Gabriel's and what came to be called Calvary Cemetery, for which land had been given in 1836. These men had not been interred in either cemetery.

But with the sporadic nature of burial records prior to 1840, another question arose based upon the documents filed with the Register in Probate. A few of the estate records were for men who had had affiliations with Protestant faiths. Were non-Catholics also buried in the cemetery consecrated by a Catholic priest? So far, no answer can be given to that question.

Probate records can only document the death of a person who owned property subject to probate. If a person died and had no property, he or she would have been quietly buried without any probate record. People without property could include men, married women, older men and women living with children, and children. So, more deaths, mostly of women and children, likely occurred at Prairie du Chien beyond what the church and probate records document.

Other sources that include legal documents, remembrances, letters, and newspaper accounts have provided information about people who died at Prairie du Chien prior to 1840 for whom there was no burial or probate record.

Though most of the burials in the cemetery are unmarked, monuments remain for four gravesites. An early 20th century photograph pictures another grave for which no church record or probate record was found. Correspondence from the 1830s discuss yet another burial. So, many sources were examined in an attempt to answer the question, "Who is buried in the Old Catholic Burying Ground?"

All of this information was checked against the lists of burials enumerated on the sign erected by the State Historical Society of Wisconsin and listed on websites. I found inaccuracies. Two and possibly three of the men who died elsewhere and were buried where they died are listed as having been buried in the Old Catholic Burying Ground. Additionally, several men whose names are also enumerated on the sign and in the lists posted on websites are buried in St. Gabriel's Cemetery.

All of the information I located pertaining to deaths and burials in the Old Catholic Burying Grounds at Prairie du Chien is contained in this work.

I begin with a short history of Prairie du Chien as it pertains to the settlement and establishment of a community on the prairie. Most of the information on Prairie du Chien in the late 18th and early 19th centuries exists in fur trade, land, and military records. Within these records are comments and short entries that offer some information on deaths at Prairie du Chien.

This history of Prairie du Chien, as it pertains to the Old Catholic Burying Ground, becomes more documented once the Catholic Church learns that communities of French-speaking people are in existence on the most northwestern portion of the Northwest Territory, and church leaders are moved with the responsibility to minister to the residents of the prairie. The Catholic priests who come to Prairie du Chien as missionaries communicated with their superiors and wrote about what they did, saw, and experienced. Additionally, newly arrived Anglo-Americans found the residents of Prairie du Chien, who spoke French and had married Native or metis women, a curiosity. Their writings about the eccentricities of the people and events on the prairie contain additional information on deaths and burials on the prairie.

From these sources, I was able to draw together many details for a history of the Old Catholic Burying Ground. This work is not meant to be a complete history of Prairie du Chien from the time of settlement by French-speaking people through the first half of the 19th century. Rather, it is the story of Prairie du Chien and the national events that affected the prairie and its residents as they pertain to and affect the history of the Old Catholic Burying Ground.

Following the history, the reader will find specific information on the burials in the Old Catholic Burying Ground. I have divided the information into parts based upon evidence of burial. The first list enumerates the documented burials in the Old Catholic Burying Ground and was developed from the records maintained by the Catholic priests who came to Prairie du Chien. The burials are listed in chronological order. The second list includes all the burials for which a headstone or a burial marker still exists. The third list is based upon deaths and information documented by the Crawford County probate records and information on deaths found in various correspondence and manuscripts. This third list therefore is a compilation of *probable* burials. The fourth list includes the names of men who the sign and the websites state are buried in the cemetery but for which there is documentation that the person is buried elsewhere. I also included information on three men not of the Catholic faith but who died during the years the Old Catholic Burying Ground was used as a place of burial.

Included with each person so listed is information (if documented) on his/her birth, baptism, marriage, death, and date of burial. There is also a biographical sketch for each person. Some sketches are longer than others.

Quite often a person's probate contained bills for expenses charged against the estate. Sometimes, the bills included information on the person's illness or burial. Any information so found will be included in the person's biographical sketch.

Michel Brisbois, one of the earliest residents of the prairie, died in 1837. He had requested that when he died, he be buried atop one of the bluffs that overlook the prairie. At the time of his death, Brisbois was interred as he wished. Upon their demise, other members of the Brisbois family were interred near Michel. The five family burials constitute the Brisbois Cemetery. A history of the Brisbois Cemetery and biographical information on the men and women buried on the bluff is also included.

As with all research, the lists are not definitive. More information may be found that proves or disproves a burial. I only have made an attempt to provide some level of accuracy to a fascinating part of Prairie du Chien's early history.

PART ONE

1774 - 1815

One of the "French Congregations"

The Catholic Church had long sought to bring Christianity to the Native nations who lived throughout North America. As French explorers traveled ever westward from the Atlantic Ocean and then along the reaches of the St. Lawrence River, through the Great Lakes to the Mississippi River, they claimed vast tracts of land for the King of France. In France, as in most European countries in the 17th and 18th centuries, there was no separation of church and state. Explorers for their country brought their faith with them and believed that their faith was the one all should practice. So, French explorers were representatives of the French government and the Roman Catholic Church. As such, a priest often traveled with the explorer; in some instances, the priest was as much an explorer as his companion. They both represented France and the Catholic Church.

To secure control of the land in North America claimed for France, the provincial governors ordered forts to be constructed at strategic locations on lakes and rivers. Within the walls of the fortification, a chapel was also erected. The Governor of New France appointed the commandant for each post. The commanding officer was to ensure not only the control of the region but also control of the fur trade for France. The Catholic Church assigned a priest to minister to the colonial regular troops and Frenchmen stationed at the post. Additionally, the priest was to go amongst the Native peoples and instruct them in the Catholic faith.

Father Claude Allouez was an early missionary to what is now Wisconsin. A member of the Society of Jesus, Allouez and other Jesuit priests were among the first European settlers in the *pays d'en haut* (upper country) of New France. Striking inland from their base in Quebec, they attempted to convert the Native people with whom they lived to Catholicism. Allouez founded the mission of *La Pointe de St. Esprit* on Madeline Island in 1665—almost twenty years before the French constructed a trading fort on the island. Father Allouez then traveled to Green Bay. He selected a site along the east bank of the Fox River and in 1671 established the mission of *St. Francis Xavier de la Baie*. In 1684, a chapel was built, and the mission operated until it was destroyed in 1687. When the French built *Fort la Baie* in 1717, the mission was reestablished within the fort and functioned until the fort was destroyed in 1760 at the end of the French and Indian War.

Jacques Marquette was also a Jesuit priest and had traveled with Louis Jolliet on the waters of the Fox and Wisconsin Rivers to reach the Mississippi River. Like his fellow priests, Marquette had hoped to bring the Catholic faith to the Native peoples he met along the voyage. Marquette and Jolliet had entered the Mississippi River just south of the prairie that would be named *la Prairie des Chiens*. After their journey, Father Marquette returned to the mission at St. Ignace.

This prairie above the confluence of the Wisconsin River with the Mississippi had long been considered a place of importance. Native people had traditionally gathered at the prairie to trade prior to the arrival of the Europeans. All tribal hostilities were set aside on the prairie, for the tribes of the upper Mississippi considered the wide expanse neutral ground. As the nations of Europe vied for dominance in the New World, the prairie gained in importance; representatives of each country knew that whoever controlled the prairie controlled the upper Mississippi River and its tributaries.

In the late 17th century, Nicolas Perrot, a French explorer and fur trader, had had a seasonal fortification constructed on the prairie. Little is known of the installation called Fort St. Nicolas. By the 1690s, French cartographers included the fort on their maps of the New World. Though of strategic importance, French colonial regular troops did not man the fort nor was a priest assigned to start a mission in conjunction with the fort. Paul Marin may have utilized fort St. Nicolas during his years of service to France. Commander at *Baie-des-Puants* (Green Bay), Marin traveled in the Mississippi Valley to maintain peace among the Dakota, Meskwaki, and Sauk, and engaged in the fur trade. In 1752, Marin's son Joseph assumed command at *Baie-des-Puants*. The following year he built a trading fort at the mouth of the Wisconsin River. Fort St. Nicolas and Marin's fort were outposts for use in the fur trade. French officers/fur traders and their employees occupied the forts. But beyond the trading forts, during in the years of French control, there was no permanent European habitation on the upper Mississippi and its tributaries. And as there were no permanent French posts along the upper Mississippi, the Catholic Church did not establish a mission on the upper Mississippi River.

In the mid-18th century, French exploration ceased, and the fur trade suffered as hostilities between France and Great Britain burgeoned into warfare. France sought to maintain control of the vast reaches it had claimed in North America, and Great Britain wanted to gain the same land and access to the furs. Great Britain won the conflict. By the Treaty of Paris of 1763, France lost all of its territory on mainland North America. Great Britain gained Canada, which included the Ohio Valley and upper Mississippi region, and also received the portion of Louisiana east of the Mississippi River. The port of New Orleans and colony of Louisiana west of the Mississippi were ceded to Spain for their efforts as a British ally.

With the end of French control, Catholic missionaries no longer journeyed the Great Lakes and western rivers. The post and mission at Green Bay had been abandoned during the French and Indian War, and the fortification constructed by Perrot at Prairie du Chien stood empty. The presence of the Jesuits, who had been the missionaries to the Indian nations in French-held territory, had declined; and once New France was under British control, Great Britain barred the immigration of Jesuit priests to North America.

Now in control of the eastern half of North America, Great Britain attempted to organize the fur trade so that only English-speaking men could participate. A rebellion, led by the Ottawa chief Pontiac, made the British realize that the fur trade, as organized by the French, worked well and was what the Native nations preferred. Within a few years, the trade in the western Great Lakes and upper Mississippi functioned once again. With Montreal now the headquarters of the British fur trade, the strategic positions of Green Bay and Prairie du Chien played an important role in the fur trade once more.

French-speaking men from Canada, the Illinois Country, and as far away as New Orleans congregated every fall and spring on the prairie. In the fall, they arrived with their canoes filled with bales of trade goods and a few casks of high wine. The wine they stored at the prairie, perhaps in the old French fort. They then sorted and reassembled their goods before splitting up into smaller brigades and paddling north to the wintering places. In spring, all gathered once again on the prairie. No matter if the trading had been good or poor, they spent several weeks camped on the prairie. The casks of wine were brought out of hiding, broached, and merriment ensued.

In the 1770s, the prairie grew to be politically as well as economically important. In the early 1770s some French-speaking men from the Illinois Country moved north with their families and settled on the prairie. In a casual method, they chose land to live upon and farm. They built homes and broke the prairie, planting wheat, barley, and rye, often selling the surplus in St. Louis.

In the early 1700s, France had established a permanent fortified settlement at Michilimackinac. French-Canadians engaged in the fur trade had made their homes at Michilimackinac, married, and started families. When Great Britain gained control of New France, the French at Michilimackinac had been joined by British Canadians. The traders and their *engagés* had seasonally gathered on the prairie, transporting their furs each spring along the Fox-Wisconsin waterway to Lake Michigan and then eastward to be sold in the British trading houses in Montreal. With the spread of the fur trade to the upper reaches of the Mississippi and the Missouri rivers, some of the French-speaking traders selected plots of land at Prairie du Chien and moved from Michilimackinac, erecting homes and trading houses on the prairie.

In 1774, the Parliament of Great Britain passed the Quebec Act. The law provided for the protection of the Roman Catholic faith. French-speaking residents of what had been French territory no longer had to take an oath of loyalty to Great Britain, and they could practice their faith freely. The act reinstated French civil law in combination with British criminal law. The act allowed all the French-speaking people living in the British colonies of Quebec and Louisiana to practice their Catholic faith. But the Catholic Church did not have the power and position it had held under French rule. No priests came to Green Bay or Prairie du Chien to minister to the residents. To have a marriage sanctified or children baptized required a trip by canoe to either Michilimackinac or St. Louis. When a person slipped into his or her last illness, no priest could be summoned to offer a final blessing or say prayers at the burial.

The methods by which Great Britain controlled the fur trade in North America and the privileges of the Catholic Church in Quebec and Louisiana only added to the dissatisfaction of the Protestant-dominant thirteen colonies towards Great Britain. Soon after the Americans at Philadelphia declared independence and established the United States of America, residents of Green Bay and Prairie du Chien were drawn into the hostilities. Then in 1780, British-backed forces under the command of Lt. Charles Gautier arrived on the prairie. They used the old French fort as the staging point for an attempted attack on American forces at St. Louis. When the attack failed, Gautier burned the fort along with the furs they could not transport to Michilimackinac. The men and families at *la Prairie des Chiens* were left to fear an attack from the Americans. The attack never happened, but some of the men with connections to St. Louis, such as Julian Dubuque and Louis Honoré, left *la Prairie des Chiens* to settle further down the Mississippi where they could maintain their economic connections to St. Louis.

The men who remained at *la Prairie des Chiens* sought security and legal protection from the British governor at Michilimackinac. In a petition, the residents requested they be given title to the prairie, which was their home and from which they gained their livelihood. In 1781, Patrick Sinclair, lieutenant governor of Quebec, purchased three tracts of land from the Indian nations gathered on Mackinac Island.

This purchase, intended for the residents, included the land along the Fox River, which constituted Green Bay, and the twelve-mile prairie of Prairie du Chien.[11]

With the close of the American Revolution, once again the land east of the Mississippi River and south of the Great Lakes passed into the control of another political entity: this time it was the United States of America. Only a small percentage of the citizens of the new United States were Catholic. During the colonial era, only the colonies of Maryland and Pennsylvania had allowed people of the Catholic faith to settle within their jurisdiction. The few priests within these colonies had come to North America from Europe. After 1763, these priests were under the authority of the Bishop of Quebec.

Father John Carroll of Maryland had been the first American to be ordained a priest, so when the Catholic Church established the first diocese in the United States in 1793, John Carroll was appointed bishop. From the office of the diocese in Baltimore, he immediately saw a need for priests to minister to the residents who had migrated from the thirteen states to land west of the Appalachian Mountains, now designated the Northwest Territory. In time, Bishop Carroll sent Father Gabriel Richard to Detroit to minister to the Catholics of that settlement and the vast region to the north and west, the home of several Native nations.

Father Richard was one of the many Catholic priests, who had left France after the beginning of the French Revolution when the National Assembly had ordered the confiscation of the property of the Catholic Church and banned religious congregations and orders in France. In 1792, Father Richard arrived in Baltimore where he was to teach at St. Mary's Seminary. But with no students in attendance, Bishop Carroll sent several priests to minister to the French-speaking residents of the Illinois Country. For six years, Father Richard worked among the residents of Kaskaskia, Cahokia, and Prairie du Rocher. In 1798, Bishop Carroll sent Father Richard to Ste. Anne's parish at Detroit. This "parish" extended from the River Raisin along the shores of the Strait of Detroit, around Lake Saint Clair and Lakes Huron and Michigan and then the Georgian Bay, up the St. Mary's River, and beyond to the western point of Lake Superior. Father Richard's parish therefore included Green Bay and Prairie du Chien. In 1799, Father Richard made his first journey to visit missions in the northern and western parts of his parish. He later wrote to Bishop Carroll that Mackinac "is a great rendezvous for traders from Lake Michigan, the Mississippi, Lake Superior, and other points." He learned of other gathering places "at St. Joseph's River, Wisconsin River, Prairie du Chien, Green Bay, Sainte Mary's Falls," and trading points along Lake Superior. While he was able to visit Saint Joseph Island and then the mission at Sault Ste. Marie, the coming of winter forced his to return to Detroit.[12]

If Father Richard had made a request for a priest to travel to Green Bay and Prairie du Chien, a lack of priests would have caused Bishop Carroll not to fulfill Father Richard's request. More priests were needed in the new United States. The Catholic population in the Northwest was increasing. In 1808, the Diocese of Baltimore was divided. The land west of the Appalachian Mountains formed the new Diocese of Bardstown, Kentucky. Rev. Joseph Flaget was appointed bishop in 1810.

Included in the Diocese of Bardstown were the State of Kentucky, the State of Tennessee, the State of Ohio, and all of the rest of the Northwest Territory. Conditions on the frontier were very unsettled. As Father Richard and Bishop Flaget stated, more and more Catholics were moving into the region. But the expansion of all settlers into the Northwest Territory was being obstructed. The Native nations who had hunted and farmed the land for generations often attacked isolated homesteads. In 1811, the Shawnee chief Tecumseh united the Indian nations to try and stop the flow of settlers into traditionally held Indian lands. The British provided military support to Tecumseh and his allies. A goal of the British was to create a "neutral Indian state" and thereby continue the fur trade.

Although the western Great Lakes and upper Mississippi Valley were part of the United States, agents of British trading houses headquartered in Montreal operated freely in this region. These men and independent British traders resided in Mackinac, Green Bay, and Prairie du Chien, many wintering in the northern reaches of Wisconsin. When the United States declared war on Great Britain in 1812, most of the residents of

Prairie du Chien and Green Bay maintained alliance with Great Britain, as their livelihood depended upon the British fur trade.

In the spring of 1814, United States troops under the direction of William Clark, Governor of Missouri Territory, established Fort Shelby at Prairie du Chien. The British at Michilimackinac organized an expedition in relief of Prairie du Chien. Composed of traders, voyageurs, and a large contingent of Native people, the men arrived in Prairie du Chien in July 1814. After a three-day siege, Fort Shelby surrendered, and Prairie du Chien remained under British protection for another year. The Treaty of Ghent ended the War of 1812, and any military or economic influence or connections the British from Canada had in the Northwest Territory ended.

With the Indians and their British allies defeated, Bishop Flaget could now address the needs of the vast diocese for which he was responsible. The war had brought to his attention Prairie du Chien and the souls living there who were in need of a priest. On April 10, 1815, Bishop Flaget wrote a report to Pope Pius VII describing the parishes within the Diocese of Bardstown that he had visited. After describing Ste. Anne's at Detroit and La Rivière aux Raisins, both of which had a priest, Bishop Flaget wrote, "Besides these, on my journey, I heard of four French congregations settled in the midst of the Indians, who belong to my diocese, one on the upper part of the Mississippi, one in the place commonly called Chicago, another on the shores of Lake Michigan, a fourth near the head of the Illinois River. But neither the time nor the war would permit me to visit them."[13]

The congregation "on the upper part of the Mississippi" was Prairie du Chien. Under Bishop Flaget's administration, a priest would finally arrive at Prairie du Chien.

1816

A New Order and Upheaval on the Prairie

The Treaty of Ghent, signed on December 24, 1814, formally established peace between the United States and Great Britain. By signing the Treaty, not only did the British desert the many Native nations that had been their allies in the conflict, Britain left the residents of Michilimackinac, Green Bay, and Prairie du Chien in a questionable position. The majority of the residents of these three communities had also been allies of Great Britain and were now left to wonder what would happen to them.

The influence of the British traders in the upper Northwest was still strong. Though the British had given up all claims to lands within the Northwest Territory with the signing of the Treaty of Ghent, individual traders at Prairie du Chien kept up their trading connections with the Montreal trading houses. Jean Baptiste Bertholet, James Aird, Joseph Rolette, François Bouthellier operated trading outfits from their houses in the Main Village. To break the hold of the British traders upon the Indians, in 1816 the United States Congress passed an act forbidding foreigners to trade on American soil. Considered "foreigners" and unable to gain a trading license from the United States, the independent traders and voyageurs living in Green Bay and Prairie du Chien contracted with agents of the American Fur Company. In the western Great Lakes, the American Fur Company continued to use Mackinac, Green Bay, and Prairie du Chien as the centers of trade.

The United States needed to gain political control of the vast region west of Lake Michigan. The War Department created a plan which included regarrisoning Fort Dearborn at Chicago, the reoccupation of Prairie du Chien, and construction of new forts at the mouth of the Fox River at Green Bay, at or near the Falls of St. Anthony, and at Rock Island. At the same time, the government fur factory at Chicago would be restored and new U.S. factories opened at Green Bay and Prairie du Chien. A U.S. Indian agency had operated at Prairie du Chien since 1808; after the end of hostilities, Nicolas Boilvin reopened the Prairie du Chien Agency in September 1815.

John W. Johnson, an experienced fur factor, was appointed as the factor to the United States Factory at Prairie du Chien. Arriving ahead of the military, Johnson pulled ashore on May 26, 1816. He assumed possession of the buildings owned by the Michilimackinac Company located in a prime position in the Main Village.

With two components of the United States plan to control the Indians and the lands of the western territories operating at Prairie du Chien, the third component arrived in June 1816. Bvt. Brig. General Thomas A. Smith, commanding the western department of the United States Army left St. Louis with six companies of the Rifle Regiment. After a stop to select the site for the placement of the new fort at Rock Island and begin its construction, Smith proceeded up the Mississippi arriving at Prairie du Chien on June 20, 1816. The following day, Smith exerted his authority.

Major Richard Graham, Indian Agent for Illinois Territory had accompanied Smith and the troops. Together Smith and Graham issued an order requiring all the traders in the village to produce their trading licenses. Congress had passed an act on April 29 in which it was stated, "licenses to trade with the Indians within the territorial limits of the United States shall not be granted to any but citizens of the United States..." Also, any goods "carried by a foreigner into the lands to which the Indian title has not been extinguished for the purpose of being used in the Indian trade" would be confiscated. The two terms that played to the advantage of Smith were "foreigner" and "lands to which the Indian title had not been extinguished." In Smith's eyes, anyone who had aided Britain in any way during the hostilities was a foreigner. Based upon their interpretation of the Act, Smith refused to recognize the licenses held by the traders at Prairie du Chien and confiscated their trade goods.[14]

One of the most prominent residents of Prairie du Chien was Michel Brisbois. Brisbois and members of his family had various connections to the British. Brisbois was an educated man of prominence, and so, Smith made him an example to the community of what would happen to British sympathizers. According to James H. Lockwood, a clerk for the American Fur Company and local resident at the time, Smith charged Brisbois with treason, "keeping him in duress for several days." Smith then ordered Brisbois placed on a boat returning to St. Louis. After Brisbois was gone, Smith confiscated the Brisbois family home and all their property. Smith then surveyed the community for the most advantageous site for the new American fort. He selected the slight mound behind some of the houses in the Main Village. Under the direction of Colonel William S. Hamilton, the soldiers started to erect the fort on July 3. It was soon named Fort Crawford in honor of Secretary of War William H. Crawford.[15]

The ground selected for Fort Crawford and its attendant needs encroached upon "the ancient burying ground" of the prairie. The term "ancient" to describe the cemetery was used by James H. Lockwood. As traders and farmers were residing on the prairie by 1774, the burials probably dated at least from this period. The burying grounds interfered with Smith's plans for the fortification. He therefore ordered the residents of the prairie to disinter their dead and remove them to another site. The site they chose for the burying ground was a piece of high ground located on the mainland.[16]

When French-speaking men and their families arrived from the Illinois Country and Michilimackinac to make a new home at Prairie du Chien, each selected a piece of land on which to build a house and outbuildings, and some acquired an additional piece of land to farm. By 1816, most of the permanent residents at the prairie owned a lot within either the Main Village, the Village of St. Friole, or the Upper

Village. The large prairie behind the villages had been partitioned into forty-three farm lots. Some of the residents had constructed homes at the edge of their farm lot. A part of each lot was cultivated, and a part was used for pasturing animals.

The first burying ground for the community had been established in the Main Village, where the majority of the residents had their homes. Now the residents had been ordered to move the buried remains of family members and friends. They decided that the new burying ground would be safer from the activities of the military post if placed on the mainland. François Vertefeuille and Augustin Hebert may have offered part of their farm lots as the location of the burying ground. The land on these two lots rose higher than surrounding farm lots, and the land was never covered by water when the Mississippi River rose.

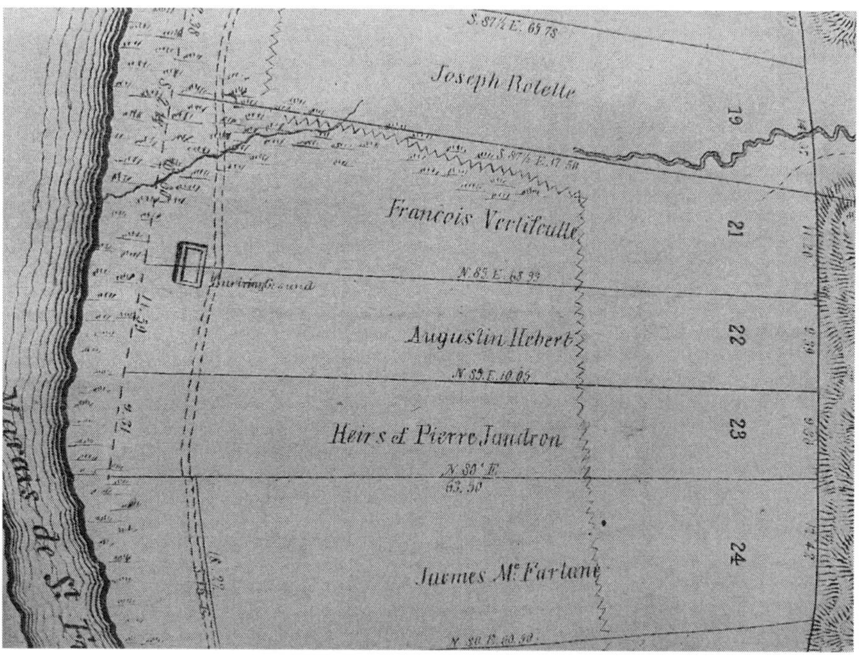

Detail from *Plat of the Private Claims at Prairie du Chien, Drawn by Lucius Lyon, U. S. Surveyor.* In 1827, Lucius Lyon did a precise survey of the village and farm lots at Prairie du Chien. A map, based upon the Lyon survey, was published by C. B. Graham. The map shows that the "burying ground" stretched across farm lots owned by François Vertefeuille and Augustin Hebert. (Villa Louis State Historic Site, Wisconsin Historical Society)

The two farm lots also stood equidistant between the Upper Village and the Village of St. Friole, and this site was easily accessible by the people who lived in the Main Village. And so, Vertefeuille gave the portion of his Farm Lot No. 21 that stood west of the "Highway" to the community for its burying ground, and Hebert did the same, offering a portion of Farm Lot No. 22.[17]

Realizing their vulnerability to United States military authority, in 1816 the inhabitants of Prairie du Chien submitted a petition to the Congress of the United States. In the petition, the residents outlined a history of the continuance of habitation on the prairie since 1755 to the present. They presented themselves as "easy and tranquil under the successive sovereignties of France, England, and the Republic of the United States..." and "had entirely omitted to secure titles to the village lots and fields which they had inhabited and cultivated for so many years." They therefore now found themselves in the position of being "expelled from their fireplaces as intruders upon the national domain; and subject to military regulations..." They therefore requested that they, the inhabitants, be confirmed in their possession of the village lots and land. The residents were facing a great problem, for they had no "bits of parchment to protect themselves" from Colonel Chambers.[18]

On April 22, 1817, Colonel Talbot Chambers arrived at Prairie du Chien to take command of Fort Crawford. Chambers saw himself not only as the commanding officer of the fort but also as the representative authority of the United States government. He instituted martial law. Looking at the fort in the midst of the Main Village, he decided changes were needed. Chambers ordered Antoine LaChapelle, James McFarlane, and Basile Giard to take down their homes and remove them to the lower end of the Village. Chambers then assessed the needs of the garrison, deciding more land was required. He commandeered the lots north of the fort and all land east of Fort Crawford to the *marais*. Again, Chambers ordered those who lived on this land to disassemble their homes and move them to the southern parts of the Village where there was vacant land. Under Colonel Chambers, thirteen families were dispossessed of their land.

Chambers chose to make an example of Joseph Rolette, who was rising to become the most important trader on the prairie. Charging Rolette with immoral conduct, Chambers banished him to an island located about seven miles above Prairie du Chien. Not until the spring of 1818 would Chambers allow Rolette to return his home in the Main Village.

Into this scene of martial law and displacement would arrive the first priest to journey to Prairie du Chien: Father Marie Joseph Dunand.

"Prairie du Chien, 1830" from *Das Mississippithal* by James Lewis.

1817

Spiritual Solace in the Midst of Martial Law

Spring of 1817 was slow to arrive. As the residents of the prairie watched the ice on the Mississippi River slowly break up, they may have wondered what the opening of the waters would bring to Prairie du Chien. To the south, Father Marie Joseph Dunand also watched the river and waited impatiently. He yearned to bring the sacraments of the Catholic Church to another group of souls in need of solace. With the coming of March, Father Dunand, a Trappist priest and pastor of St. Ferdinand de Florissant near St. Louis, decided it was time to begin his journey to Prairie du Chien.

The Order of Cistercians of the Strict Observance, or Trappists, had existed since the 17th century. The French Revolution had closed all the Trappist monasteries in France, and the monks retreated to Switzerland. With the loss of their monastery, Dom Augustin de Lastrange, the abbot of the order, sent small groups of monks to minister in other countries across Europe. It had long been his wish to establish a monastery in America, and in 1803 the first group of Trappists arrived in the United States. A second group of six men followed in 1805, led by Father Marie Joseph Dunand.

Arriving in Baltimore, the six men joined Father Urbain Guillet, who had left France with twenty-seven monks three years previously and was the Trappist Superior in North America. Remaining only a few days, the seven men departed for Bardstown, Kentucky where the first group of Trappists had settled at the invitation of Father Stephen Badin. The trip and life in the unsettled reaches of Kentucky were severe, and many of the monks, unused to the primitive conditions, died. Father Dunand, having been a grenadier during the French Revolution, was hardened to living in the elements with little food. A few months after arriving at Bardstown, Father Dunand and the others left to begin a monastery on Casey Creek, located about fifty miles south of Bardstown. The Trappists acquired 800 acres and established a farm with a sawmill. They began to offer an education and instruction in manual skills to the children of the residents of Casey County. The students could board at the farm, with all expenses borne by the monks. The monastery burnt down in 1808, and the following year Father Dunand and the monks left Kentucky, walking to Kaskaskia in Illinois territory, crossing the frozen Mississippi River and then walking on to St. Louis in Missouri Territory. There, Father Dunand oversaw the construction of a church and then traveled between Illinois and Missouri as missionary to many. The monks who had traveled with Father Dunand purchased a farm in Looking Glass Prairie, Territory of Illinois, and built temporary cabins. They had wished to minister to the Native people who lived in the area, but disease and hardship reduced the members of the community, and in 1813, all the monks but three chose to return to France. Father Dunand chose to remain and committed to care for the congregation on the west side of the Mississippi River; he resided at St. Charles.[19]

While in St. Louis or at Portage des Sioux where he was ministering to the Native people, Father Dunand met a resident of Prairie du Chien. That person (name unknown) invited him to come to Prairie du Chien and offer Mass. He must have explained to Dunand the number of people at the prairie wishing a blessing on their marriages and baptisms for their children. Father Dunand determined to visit them.[20]

As March of 1817 arrived in St. Louis, Father Dunand began his trip up the Mississippi. According to Father Dunand's diary, he engaged six men, five to paddle and one to steer the canoe. He "bargained" to pay them one hundred and ten francs a month "for they would have many difficulties to overcome." Dunand knew the men would be paddling against "frequent winds" and have to endure extreme cold. He had engaged a large canoe, for Father Dunand would sit in the middle of the canoe, surrounded by provisions, gifts for any Indians they might encounter, and the vestments, missal, chalice, and all else he needed to say Mass and administer the sacraments.[21]

The trip was more harrowing than Father Dunand surmised. They had hardly begun the trip when a heavy snow started to fall and quickly covered the land. Ice still clung to the river shores, and as each day grew colder the river began to freeze. The paddles were soon covered with ice, and they "scarcely touched the water" forcing the men to pull to shore. They waited several days for conditions to improve so that they could continue. On the river once more, they progressed a hundred leagues only to face another obstacle. As the boatmen navigated the rapids where the Des Moines River flowed into the Mississippi, Dunand feared they all might perish. Each night on their journey, the men paddled the canoe to shore and set up camp close to the riverbank. And each night Native men and their families visited them. They, too, felt the cold and came to warm themselves around the fire tended by the boatmen. Once warmed, the chiefs and leaders offered Dunand their hand in greeting. To all, Father Dunand offered gifts of tobacco that "greatly pleased them." Then, Father Dunand wrote, "The thirty-fourth day from the time of my departure after great fatigue and hardships we reached the place to which we sought to carry the light of faith." As soon as his canoe touched the shore, news of his arrival spread across the prairie. Father Dunand wrote that he was "heartily welcomed" by the residents of Prairie du Chien, and he quickly set about his mission.[22]

The exact date of Father Dunand's arrival at Prairie du Chien is not known. He only recorded, "The thirty-fourth day from the time of my departure" he and the boatmen arrived at the prairie. The record of the sacraments he administered while at Prairie du Chien is more detailed with dates recorded. The first page or two of his record has been lost, so the document begins with his record of the sixth baptism performed. Alex St. Syre (Cyr) was the sixth person that Father Dunand baptized in April 1817. And as the twelfth baptism, that of Alexandre Periard, occurred on April 22, it can be assumed Dunand arrived at Prairie du

Chien several days before April 22.[23]

When Father Dunand arrived at the prairie, he later wrote, "the Commander of the fort [Colonel Talbot Chambers] although a Protestant, honored me with a visit." Chambers offered Dunand accommodations within a structure that was part of Fort Crawford, and Father Dunand wrote that he accepted the colonel's offer. On May 10, Colonel Chambers reported that "a Roman Catholic Priest" had prevented Robert Dickson from attending a dance. Apparently, Dunand was attempting to institute some moral control over the residents under his spiritual guidance.[24]

Father Dunand "lived one month among" the residents, whom he felt "had been entirely abandoned" by the Catholic Church. In recalling his stay on the prairie, Dunand wrote that each day was spent "in the exercise of the holy ministry." He instructed Protestants and people of the Jewish faith in the teachings of the Catholic Church. He marveled that the Native people attended Mass, which he offered daily, the women bringing their children that they "might behold a Makita Courage; that is to say a black-robe who speaks to the Master of Life." Some of the women asked that their children be baptized.[25]

Each day Father Dunand offered Holy Mass for the residents of the prairie and the Native people who wished to attend. He offered the Sacraments of Holy Eucharist and Penance, and then dedicated much of each day to ministering to the needs of the community. Dunand stated he "administered holy Baptism to a great many, large and small...." The extant written record maintained by Father Dunand details that he administered the Sacrament of Baptism to one hundred and thirty-five people. In each entry, he recorded the date of the baptism and the name of the person baptized, citing either the person's age or birth date, the person's parents, and the name of the person's godfather and godmother. Dunand devoted the first few days entirely to the administration of baptism. Some days as many as fifteen people were baptized. Almost all of the people listed as having received the Sacrament of Baptism were children, the sons and daughters of French-speaking parents who had lived many years on the prairie and who had been brought up in the Catholic faith. Several members of the

Bart, Giard, and Peltier families were in their twenties when baptized by Father Dunand. As to the instructions he gave to people of other faiths, the only Protestants he mentioned baptizing were the three children of Robert Dickson and a Dakota woman [To-To-Win]. As to those of the Jewish faith, one boy was baptized, his father listed as "Juda Joseph, a Jew." According to the extant records of Dunand's ministry at Prairie du Chien, the only Native person brought into the Catholic faith through baptism was Catherine, a Fox woman, who was fifty-one years old.[26]

On some days, between baptisms, Dunand performed marriages. The marriage records are even more detailed. He recorded the date of the marriage, the names of the couple, the parents of the bride and groom, and often the place of birth of the bride or groom. For each marriage, Dunand required that at least two people stand as witness for the groom and the bride; their signatures are part of the record. In all, fourteen marriages were performed.[27]

In the month Father Dunand spent at Prairie du Chien, he officiated at one burial. On May 10, he buried a man whose name was recorded as Grand LaJour, "his baptismal name unknown." This was the only burial to occur while Father Dunand was at the prairie. As a Catholic priest, Dunand would not officiate at a burial in unconsecrated ground, so he took this opportunity to bless "the parish cemetery" and did so on May 10, 1817.[28] "The parish cemetery" came to be called the Old Catholic Burying Ground.

Often Colonel Chambers conducted councils with the leaders of the Native nations. The gatherings took place in the structure in which Father Dunand resided during his stay. Chambers therefore invited Dunand to attend the councils. The councils began "immediately after dinner," and Dunand attended several times, staying but "a few minutes." He was fascinated by the ritual that opened each council and recorded the details of lighting and smoking the pipe.[29]

After about five weeks in Prairie du Chien, Father Dunand left the community and returned to Missouri. In his time at the prairie, Dunand performed 135 baptisms and sanctified fourteen marriages, blessed the "parish cemetery," and officiated at one burial. He continued his mission work in Missouri until 1820, when he returned to France.[30]

Several years after his return to France, Father Dunand was asked to write about the years he spent in North America. In his memoir, he recounts the hardships he and his fellow monks faced as they lived in missions in Kentucky and Illinois. He told stories of men in sin whom he directed to a better life. He was fascinated by the culture of the Native people he met, and minutely described dress, ceremonies, and cultural practices of various tribes. Dunand wrote in detail about the rituals he witnessed at the councils held at Fort Crawford. Conversely, other than general statements about his ministrations to the residents of Prairie du Chien, he did not record any details or stories concerning any individual residing on the prairie.[31]

Signature of Father Marie Joseph Dunand of the Order of Reformed Cistercians or Trappists.

1827 - 1829

Rev. François Vincent Badin

Father Dunand had carefully made a written record of baptisms, marriages, and the one burial he had administered at Prairie du Chien. This record seemed to have remained at Prairie du Chien and was entrusted to the care of someone living in the community. Whoever became responsible for the preservation of the document was not a Catholic priest. There is no subsequent chronicling or notes of any baptisms or marriages being blessed. But after the entry by Father Dunand of the burial of Grand Lajour, there are sixteen entries for burials that occurred from June 6, 1817, through September 20, 1825, all after he left the prairie. The entries are very brief. Each entry identifies the name of the deceased and the date of burial. Four entries include additional information on the deceased. Apparently, more than one person was responsible for recording the events, for the notations are written in different handwriting.[32]

The record, though, was not assiduously maintained. The entries appended to Father Dunand's record are not a complete documentation of the deaths that occurred and the subsequent burials in the "parish cemetery" at Prairie du Chien. Seven burials were listed as occurring during the years of 1817, 1818, and 1819. Then, there is a four-year gap from 1819 to 1823. Fours burial are listed for 1823, three for 1824, and three for 1825. With the burial of Angelle Rolette on September 20, 1825, this early record ends.

In the years after the departure of Father Dunand, the population of the community on the prairie grew. According to the U.S. Federal census, 238 people lived at Prairie du Chien in 1810. Ten years later the number rose to 351, not including soldiers stationed at Fort Crawford.[33] Prairie du Chien stood at the entrance to the upper Mississippi and its tributaries and the traditional lands of many Native nations. Prairie du Chien's location made it the perfect setting for the United States government to secure the Indian lands and open the region to white settlement.

In 1825, a treaty council with representatives of over twelve Native nations of the upper Mississippi drainage convened at Prairie du Chien. Conducted by Governor William Clark and Governor Lewis Cass, representing the United States, the resulting Treaty of Prairie du Chien was an attempt by U.S. government officials to create harmony amongst the tribes and peace between the tribes and citizens of the United States. To some, the treaty was seen as a prelude to opening the Native lands for settlement. Soon after the signing of the treaty, speculators from New York began to buy the rich prairie farmland from the French-speaking owners and to partition cultivated land into lots and blocks, hoping to gain wealth in sales to settlers soon to be arriving from the eastern United States.

Since the formation the Diocese of Bardstown, vast numbers of Catholic families had settled in Ohio, Indiana, Illinois, and Michigan. The Catholic Church responded by partitioning the Diocese of Bardstown, with the northern portion becoming the Diocese of Cincinnati. Prairie du Chien became part of the Diocese of Cincinnati.

When they left Baltimore in 1805, Father Dunand and his fellow Trappists had ended their arduous journey at Bardstown and had spent several days at a mission begun by Father Stephen Theodore Badin.

Stephen Badin was born in Orleans, France in 1768. Educated at Montaigne College, Paris, he entered the Sulpician Seminary in Orleans in 1789. That same year economic, political, and social pressures in France erupted and citizens revolted against the nobility and clergy of France. The new National Assembly of France began to enact social and economic reform. The Assembly soon declared that the Church was "at the disposal of the nation." Monastic vows were abolished, and on February 13, 1790, all religious orders were dissolved. Clergy were required to take an oath of loyalty to the nation, the law, and the king, and to support the constitution decreed by the National Assembly and accepted by the king. Those who refused would be exiled, deported, or executed.

Under this legislation, the seminary in Orleans was closed. Choosing to continue his studies, Badin left France with two priests for the United States. They arrived in Baltimore in March 1792. Badin continued his studies with the Sulpician order and was ordained a priest in May 1793. He was the first man to be ordained a Catholic priest in the United States. Bishop Carroll presented him with his first assignment in the Mission of Kentucky.

For over twenty-five years, Badin attended to the spiritual needs of various settlements in Kentucky. Then in the spring of 1819 he returned to France. Restrictions against the Catholic Church had ended in 1801, and Father Badin assumed the duties of a parish priest in a community about forty miles from Orleans.

Father Stephen Badin must have visited his family when he returned to France. Perhaps this is when his younger brother, François Vincent Badin, began his studies to become a priest. Or perhaps the manuscript that Father Stephen Badin worked on while in France swayed François. Published in 1822 as *Etat des missions du Kentucky*, Stephen may have convinced François of the need for priests in the United States.[34]

The younger Badin brother, François Vincent, felt a calling to become a missionary to the Native people of the United States. François studied for the priesthood and then continued his studies in the United States. Like his brother, the younger Badin traveled to Baltimore then on to Kentucky. There he met the Reverend Edward Fenwick. In January 1822, Fenwick was consecrated bishop of the newly created Diocese of Cincinnati, and in March he set out for Cincinnati. Three priests and François Vincent Badin accompanied Fenwick. Soon after their arrival, Bishop Fenwick ordained François Badin—the first man to be ordained a Catholic priest in Ohio.

The new Diocese of Cincinnati included Michigan Territory. Since Father François Badin was a Frenchman, Fenwick discerned that he could more ably serve the Church in Detroit where the vast majority of residents spoke French. The new Father Badin traveled to Detroit with Father Gabriel Richard, the pastor of St. Anne's Parish. The Ottawa and Pottawatomi nations had long solicited Father Richard to send them a "black gown," and so in 1824, Father Richard sent Father François Badin to minister to them. During this time, the young Father Badin traveled bringing the sacraments to various communities, including Green Bay. From 1825 into 1827, he ministered to the residents of Mackinac. Father François Badin had returned to Detroit when he received word of his new assignment. He was to visit Prairie du Chien and the Fever River.[35]

Little detail exists of Father François Vincent Badin's life as a missionary. He did not write a memoir like Father Dunand or Father Samuel Mazzuchelli, who would follow Badin as missionary to the people who lived along Lake Michigan and the Mississippi River. His correspondence is scattered, and little relates to his visits to Prairie du Chien. But Father Badin made two visits to the prairie, both several months in length. He was at Prairie du Chien for a longer period than either Father Dunand or Father Mazzuchelli. The careful records he kept of his sacramental work are the best documentation of his life on the upper Mississippi.

Father François Badin set out for Prairie du Chien in the spring of 1827, traveling first to St. Louis then up the Mississippi River. He arrived at the prairie in mid-May. He immediately saw to the spiritual needs of the community. On May 29, he baptized Marie Nessouachokachie, an Ottawa, and the young children, Henry Fisher and Charles and Alexis Pizanne.[36]

There was some confusion on Father Badin's part as to whether Prairie du Chien and the Fever River were under the jurisdiction of the Diocese of St. Louis or the new Diocese of Detroit. He therefore made his first communication about his work at Prairie du Chien to a priest in St. Louis. In a letter dated June 9, in the "third week since my arrival," he recounted that he "had much work to do." This did not surprise him "for since the time of the Jesuits, that is, since time immemorial, no priest, save the good Trappist Prior [Dunand], made his appearance at Prairie du Chien." Badin was kept "very busy" instructing thirty-six men and boys and forty-six girls and women so that they could receive their first communion. He left it to his correspondent to "imagine how great the number of invalid marriages is, and how many baptisms had to be conferred."[37]

The residents of Prairie du Chien appreciated the presence of Father Badin even though he was critical of the marital status of many of the couples. Civil government had been established at Prairie du Chien in 1818 when the prairie became part of Michigan Territory. Justices of the peace had been appointed. By the time of Father Badin's arrival at the prairie, over forty couples of French-Canadian heritage had been married in civil ceremonies by either Nicolas Boilvin or James H. Lockwood, who were justices of the peace.[38]

Father Badin was concerned whether couples married by a justice of the peace could receive the sacraments, so he wrote to Bishop Rosati at St. Louis. The Bishop responded that if Catholics were married in a civil ceremony because no priest was present, they "can be admitted to the sacraments."[39]

In early June, some of the men left the prairie to travel to an area of the river where tall trees grew. They commenced cutting trees, trimming them, and floating them with the river currants to the prairie. They planned to hew the trees into logs and erect a chapel fifty feet in length. Badin prayed, "God grant that I may be able to bless it to His greater glory before I leave the Prairie."[40]

Father Badin continued his spiritual work at Prairie du Chien until August 27, when he left for Galena. Though distressed at the lack of legitimate marriages, Father Badin only married nine couples during his first three months at the prairie. Conversely, he baptized eighty-four people, most of whom were children.[41]

Though no priest had attended upon the residents of the prairie for ten years, the settlement had not been a spiritual wasteland as

Father Badin may have led his correspondent to believe. Badin kept detailed records of each baptism he conferred, noting parents and godparents. He also recorded the date of the person's birth along with the date of the baptism. If other spiritual facts were known, these he also recorded. Of the eighty-four people baptized during the summer of 1827, Father Badin noted that fifty-seven of the children he baptized had been privately baptized soon after their birth by a resident of the prairie. One of the men may have maintained a record of the baptisms for Father Badin to have been so well informed of their spiritual work.[42]

Father Dunand had revitalized the Catholic faith of the residents of Prairie du Chien. One or more of the residents of the prairie had maintained a loose record of burials in the parish cemetery after Dunand's departure. Dunand must have also reinforced the importance of baptism. According to the teachings of the Catholic Church at that time, should a person die without being baptized, they would not be able to attain heaven. This teaching, reiterated by Father Dunand and combined with the fragility of life, taught all at the prairie of the need to baptize a child soon after its birth. Within the Catholic community of Prairie du Chien, the practice of baptizing newborn children began soon after Father Dunand left the prairie in May 1817. Father Badin noted that Joseph Mercier baptized Denis Cherrier, who had been born November 14, 1817.[43]

From 1817 until the arrival of Father Badin, fourteen different men privately baptized children born at Prairie du Chien. It was the practice to baptize children soon after they were born, a practice that Father Badin noted in two of the baptisms he conferred in 1828. So, one may assume that these men baptized the children soon after their births, the dates of which Father Badin recorded. Some men baptized only one or two children. But the responsibility of ensuring the children of Prairie du Chien would not die unbaptized fell mainly to two men. Denis Courtois had baptized thirty-two of the children, and Michel Brisbois eleven children. One of those men likely maintained the record of the baptisms.[44]

Michel Brisbois and Denis Courtois were men of importance within the French-speaking community at Prairie du Chien. Both had lived on the prairie for many years, and both could read and write. Brisbois lived in the Main Village, while Courtois lived at the north end of the prairie.

Father Badin stayed at Prairie du Chien until the last days of August 1827. He had not planned to remain at the prairie that long as he considered himself a "traveling missionary." But the events of June 28, he wrote, "constrained me to stay there against my will."[45]

Father Badin had been sent to care for the sacramental needs of the residents of Prairie du Chien and the men and families who lived along the Fever River in Illinois. Since before the arrival of Europeans, the Sauk and the Ho-Chunk had mined surface lead found in deposits along the Fever River, on land north of the river, and across the Mississippi River along Catfish Creek. The Native people would trade the lead in exchange for manufactured goods. The rich deposits attracted White men to the region, and in 1822, the United States began to grant mining leases. Some of the leases were located on land that the Ho-Chunk had never ceded to the United States. As the population in the lead mining district grew, more men came from Missouri and the eastern United States and opened pitches on Ho-Chunk land; but the United States ignored the protests of the Ho-Chunk leaders. Then in the spring of 1827, the rumor spread among the Dakota and Ho-Chunk that U.S. soldiers stationed at Fort Snelling had killed two Ho-Chunk men being held as prisoners. The sense of injustice was so great that some Ho-Chunk leaders wanted retribution.

Red Bird of the Prairie Lacrosse band of Ho-Chunk was told to go to Prairie du Chien and take two American lives to offset the two Ho-Chunk men rumored to have been killed by the Americans. Reluctantly, Red Bird accepted the directive. He, along with his son and two other men, traveled to Prairie du Chien. Not finding the Americans whom they sought in the village, the four men continued their journey to the south end of the prairie where Thomas McNair lived. Before arriving at the McNair residence, Red Bird and his companions stopped at the home of Regis Gagnier. Gagnier and Solomon Leipcap, who worked for

Gagnier, were killed. The four Ho-Chunk men then left the prairie.

The same day, June 28, a band of Ho-Chunk ambushed two keelboats near the mouth of the Bad Axe River. Under the command of Captain Alan Lindsey, the two boats were returning to St. Louis, having just delivered supplies to the troops stationed at Fort Snelling. When the two keelboats with dead and wounded aboard arrived at Prairie du Chien, the residents of the prairie, who had taken refuge in a tavern owned by Jean Brunet, formed a militia. These men reinforced some of the buildings of Fort Crawford, which the U.S. Army had abandoned in September 1826. News of the two attacks quickly spread. The men and families working the mining deposits fled their pitch to find safety at Galena.

When he arrived at Prairie du Chien, Father Badin had secured the large hall of the fort hospital as his residence and established "a pretty chapel" at one end. The space was one of the few locations within the wooden fort structures that did not have a roof that leaked or a rotten floor, so the hospital hall became crowded when the residents of the prairie sought protection in case of additional attacks. To calm all, Father Badin "sang several High Masses."[46]

Father Badin admitted his own fear, telling his superior, "I was filled with terror more than once, more than twenty times; not that I am timid, not that I am afraid of death, which, on the contrary, I desire, if it please Divine Providence, but . . .." Father Badin had to overcome his fear and fulfill the spiritual needs of Regis Gagnier.[47]

Father Badin recorded the first burial that he blessed at Prairie du Chien.

> FRANÇOIS REGIS GAGNIER, 30 years of age, killed by the Indians yesterday about noon, was buried in the cemetery of this parish by the undersigned priest, June 29, 1827, in the presence of John Simson and Augustin Hebert, who were not able to sign as required. Fran. Vit. Badin, Priest +. (Translated from French)[48]

The residents continued to use the fort buildings for their protection, and Father Badin wrote to Bishop Rosati complaining that he "was forced to move the altar more than six times, either on account of the war, or of pouring rain." The crowded living conditions may have led to the death of a mother and her son. On July 18, Father Badin blessed the burials of Marie Blondeau, about fifty-eight years old, the wife of Denis Courtois, and Denis Courtois, age twenty-eight, the son of Denis Courtois and Marie Blondeau. They had died the evening before, within a half hour of each other.[49]

Until the end of August, Father Badin was kept busy instructing boys and girls and adults in the teachings of the Catholic Church in preparation for receiving the Sacrament of Baptism. With troops once again stationed at Fort Crawford—a company of mounted volunteers under Henry Dodge protecting Galena—and General Atkinson on the way to the portage to join a force under Major William Whistler, the residents of both communities returned to their homes. Father Badin felt it was safe to depart Prairie du Chien for Galena.

Father Badin returned to Prairie du Chien in August 1828 and spent the winter on the prairie. Once again, he baptized many people, though this time the vast majority were infants who had been born after his departure the year before and were born during his stay at Prairie du Chien. He happily married young couples "according to the rites of the Church" in the presence of witnesses. And death was part of life. Badin offered "Prayers for the Dead" for two children and four adults during his second visit to Prairie du Chien. All were buried "in the parish cemetery" in the presence of witnesses. In mid-June 1829, Father Badin left Prairie du Chien.[50]

1830 - 1840

Spiritual Promises but No Continuity

As early as 1821, Bishop William DuBourg of St. Louis had wished to send missionaries to teach the faith and offer schooling to various Native people who lived in Missouri Territory. In January 1823, DuBourg was in Washington City and secured an appointment with John C. Calhoun, Secretary of War. The War Department was responsible for the administration of any affairs pertaining to the Native Nations, or Indian Affairs. DuBourg explained his plan to Calhoun, who then discussed DuBourg's proposal with President James Monroe. Both Calhoun and Monroe approved DuBourg's plan to send missionaries to Native people living in Missouri, and they promised that the United States "will contribute $200 annually towards the support of each missionary whom you may send out." DuBourg had asked for support for three missionaries; Calhoun responded that the United States would support four missionaries. The four locations to which DuBourg hoped to send missionaries were St. Louis, Council Bluffs, St. Pierre, and Prairie du Chien. He told Calhoun, "When the latter circumstance is fully ascertained, I will have the honor of addressing you for an extension of patronage."[51]

It took several years before a missionary for the Native people would be selected to go to Prairie du Chien. Joseph Rosati had replaced William DuBourg as Bishop of St. Louis, and Father François Vincent Badin had visited Prairie du Chien twice. But Father Badin had only ministered to the residents of the prairie, not the Native people who lived near Prairie du Chien.

On September 3, 1830, Bishop Rosati appointed Father Joseph Anthony Lutz to "preach the Word of God and administer the sacraments in the countries adjoining the Upper Mississippi." Father Lutz regarded himself and his mission somewhat romantically. He felt he had been called and was specially fitted for work among the Native nations.[52]

Father Lutz traveled by steamboat to Galena, arriving by the end of September. On October 8, he wrote a letter to Bishop Rosati filled with discouraging thoughts. There were few French people living at Galena; most of the residents were Irish and insisted Father Lutz preach in English. Only at Gratiot's Grove did he hope for any success in his work. He planned to visit Peoria and Sangamon City and then return to St. Louis. Though Prairie du Chien was supposed to have been the center of his work, he had not made it to the prairie and offered these excuses:

> According to your advice, I wrote a letter to them and asked them to send a man with a horse to conduct me there. It is absolutely impossible for a newcomer to travel alone in this country. Otherwise I should have had to hire a horse, an affair of twelve to fourteen dollars. Having waited one week, I decided to go there by steamboat. The "Red Rover," I was told, was to go there without fail. When it arrived here, it changed its plan, and there I was, disappointed. Not to disarrange the schedule of this present trip, I, in the little wisdom which I may possess, decided not to go there, so much the more because the place is known to me in a very unfavorable manner.... The choice of the ground plot [center of work] has been made according to your wishes, but not at Prairie du Chien.[53]

Father Lutz found Galena "more worthy of attention than Prairie du Chien."[54]

In 1831, Lutz made a second attempt to travel to Prairie du Chien and establish a mission among the Native people. He arrived in April and decided to set up a tent on the Wisconsin River about a half mile from a Menominee encampment. One night soon after his arrival, he was walking by the shore of the river when he heard the splash of paddles but thought nothing of the sound. He had just returned to his camp when he heard gunshots and loud cries. A contingent of Meskwaki had attacked the Menominee camp, killing thirty people. Lutz felt war was inevitable, which would "cause new obstacles to the spread of the Gospel." The priest returned to Galena and never attempted to be a missionary to Prairie du Chien.[55]

The next priest to minister to the residents of Prairie du Chien was Father Samuel Charles Mazzuchelli. Mazzuchelli had been born in Milan, Italy. At the age of seventeen, he entered the Dominical Order. Bishop Edward Fenwick, a fellow Dominican and head of the Diocese of Cincinnati, came to Rome in 1828 seeking young men to come to the United States and help with missions he wished to open in the further reaches of the Northwest Territory. Mazzuchelli, not yet ordained, asked permission to travel with Bishop Fenwick for he believed the "most excellent and meritorious duties of the priesthood" were to bring the Catholic faith to people "who do not know it." That same year, Mazzuchelli arrived in North America to serve in the Diocese of Cincinnati, Ohio, which at that time covered the state of Ohio and Michigan Territory, including what is now Wisconsin, Minnesota, North and South Dakotas, and Iowa. While serving in Cincinnati, Bishop Fenwick ordained Mazzuchelli.[56]

Samuel Charles Mazzuchelli, O.P. left Italy to be a missionary priest. Between 1831 and 1852, Father Mazzuchelli founded several parishes in the Illinois-Wisconsin-Iowa tri-state area and established schools. In 1832, he visited Prairie du Chien for the first time. As a result of his visits, the parish of St. Gabriel's was founded and construction of a church begun. (Sinsinawa Dominican Archives)

Following his ordination to the priesthood in 1830, Father Mazzuchelli was sent to Mackinac Island, where he served the Indigenous, American, and French-Canadian populations. While assigned to Mackinac Island, Father Mazzuchelli was often away at various missions sited along Lake Huron and Lake Michigan, traveling in all weather conditions as far as Green Bay. At Green Bay, Father Mazzuchelli had a church constructed and opened a small school. At Green Bay, he would routinely serve the Ho-Chunk and Menominee people, from which he received many converts to the Catholic faith.

In 1832, Father Mazzuchelli was ordered to visit Prairie du Chien, which the priest described as "inhabited at that time by more than six hundred persons, most of them Catholics in name only." He left Green Bay in the company of Justice James Duane Doty, arriving at the prairie on September 22. Mazzuchelli remained at Prairie du Chien until the beginning of November. He had learned from United States officials at Green Bay that "Prairie will become an important place in the new Territory; so our efforts are more demanded to make a good congregation while we can make it without opposition." To help in this effort, Father Mazzuchelli worked at "procuring a house for next spring to answer for a temporary chapel." He succeeded in acquiring "a large abandoned wooden house," and during the few weeks of his stay, Mazzuchelli used the building to say Mass and offer the sacraments.[57]

Though disappointed that more people did not show "true signs of contrition," Mazzuchelli noted he baptized "a great many children," and a "number" of couples renewed the "solemn promises of matrimony which they had already contracted according to civil law." Regrettably, Father Mazzuchelli kept no record of whom he baptized nor marriages he blessed.[58]

Kept busy at Green Bay and working among the Menominee and Ho-Chunk, Father Mazzuchelli did not return to Prairie du Chien until February 1835. Mazzuchelli found the residents "better disposed to frequent the church and the sacraments than they had been in 183[2]." Once again, Mazzuchelli remained at the prairie for only a few weeks. He baptized not only residents of Prairie du Chien but some Menominee and Chippewa; but there is no record of the names of the persons baptized. He visited Michel Brisbois in March of that year, bringing him the sacrament of Holy Eucharist. Brisbois had lapsed from the Catholic faith, and "crowds of people knelt in the room and outside the house, praying for the poor blind man whose words and edifying demeanor moved them to tears of compassion and joy."[59] While at the prairie, Mazzuchelli started an association for the building of a church. The men were to pay fifty cents a month and the women twenty-five cents a month to raise funds for the construction of the structure.[60]

By May 1835, Mazzuchelli arrived in Dubuque, having visited Mineral Point and Galena. He immediately knew that Dubuque "was destined to become a city of great importance because of its location." Mazzuchelli determined that he "could do nothing more becoming and useful to religion than to devote all his energy to the erection of a church and the formation of a parish" in that community. By August, enough money had been donated so that the foundation of a church at Dubuque was begun.[61]

Father Mazzuchelli soon began the steps to acquire land for the construction of a church in Galena and then focused once again on Prairie du Chien. He arrived at the prairie in February 1836, "augmenting the small amount of good that had been achieved there the year before."[62]

During this stay, he baptized children that had been born since his last visit in 1835. These baptisms he recorded in the "Book of Baptisms" maintained at St. Michael's Church in Galena, Illinois.[63]

During his stay, he may have preached about the need to build a church at the third of the parishes for which he was responsible. Strange and Euphrosine Antaya Powers heeded his message. On February 16, 1836, Powers sold a tract of land to Bishop Frederic Rese of the Diocese of Detroit. For one dollar, Powers sold a portion of Farm Lot No. 28, which he and his wife owned. The tract was bounded on the west by the road that passed in front of the Court House and was 360 feet square. The church structure that Mazzuchelli wished to build at Prairie du Chien would be located on this land. After celebrating Easter, Mazzuchelli left the prairie somewhat miffed that more of the residents had not received the sacraments. He attributed their indifference to "the wandering life they lead in constant association with non-Catholics."[64]

Father Mazzuchelli found more response to his preaching in Dubuque and was totally dedicated to his work in that community. In July 1836, he wrote to Bishop Rosati in St. Louis:

> For many good reasons I abandon the missions of Prairie du Chien, Fort Winnebago; and I wish to see Bishop Rese in the ends of his diocese. The 3 Liguorian priests of Green Bay, with about $3,000.00, got the possession of an establishment that cost $8,000.00, and is now worth at least $12,000.00. They have but one settlement to attend. I do not see why they should be left there in peace. Prairie du Chien and Fort Winnebago could be made part of their parish. I have to notify you, that I have received several invitations to visit the new towns below Galina [*sic*] on both sides of the Mississippi, in order to build chapels, but I cannot move from these parishes now."[65]

But Bishop Rosati did not assign other priests to minister to Prairie du Chien, and Father Mazzuchelli did not abandon the mission at Prairie du Chien completely. He had drawn plans for the church he hoped to see be constructed on the prairie.

With the construction of St. Raphael's in Dubuque rapidly progressing and the increase in the population at Dubuque and Galena, Pope Gregory XVI created the Diocese of Dubuque in July 1837. The Pope named Mathias Loras as the bishop. Bishop Loras arrived at Dubuque in 1839, after traveling throughout Europe seeking priests and funds for the new diocese.

In the summer of 1839, as the church at Dubuque was still under construction, Bishop Loras and Rev. Anthony Pelamourgues traveled up the Mississippi, stopping first at Prairie du Chien and then St. Peter on the Minnesota River. Upon their return trip, Bishop Loras and Father Pelamourgues stopped again at Prairie du Chien. The Cincinnati newspaper *Wahrheits-Freund* described all that Bishop Loras accomplished at the prairie.

> The good people of that place which is so beautifully situated at a junction of the Wisconsin and Mississippi rivers, were greatly delighted to see a Bishop in their midst for the first time. They

> earnestly sought that he tarry with them several days. So it befell, and a series of spiritual exercises, coupled with a thorough course of instructions, was begun at once.... 86 persons were led to the table of the Lord, 52 were confirmed, 19 were baptized, and 14 marriages were blessed. On a Sunday, after divine services in a house which served as a chapel, a procession was arranged which moved in a long column toward an open and elevated place, where on the ground of two acres which Mr. Pause [Powers] had given the congregation the cornerstone of a church was laid. ...The church is to be begun at once, is to be 100 feet long, 50 feet wide, and of Gothic style.

Bishop Loras dedicated the church to the Archangel Gabriel. He then returned to Dubuque. Father Pelamourgues remained at the prairie for a month.[66]

Most of the people baptized by Bishop Loras were infants and young children, but Bishop Loras also baptized Alexis Gardepie, who was eighteen years old, and Michel Labatte, who had been born in 1825. He recorded the details of the baptisms, confirmations, and marriages in the records of St. Raphael's Church upon his return to Dubuque. There is no mention of the blessing of any burial or burials.[67]

The winter passed, and in the spring of 1840, Father Mazzuchelli once again made the trip from Dubuque to Prairie du Chien. Construction on St. Gabriel's Church had resumed, and Mazzuchelli felt it necessary to be on site to direct the work and "urge people to contribute the essential materials and thus diminish the cost." By this date, at least eighty-eight individuals had made contributions towards the construction of the church with gifts ranging from one to one hundred dollars—the most generous donor being Joseph Rolette.[68]

Father Mazzuchelli worked with the men and women for "a number of days in June," even helping to quarry the limestone from which the church was being made. The parish had little financial resources, and so Bishop Loras contributed fourteen hundred dollars from the Propagation of the Faith fund that he administered. This helped to make the structure secure and usable, though not complete. This summer visit was the last time Father Mazzuchelli traveled to the prairie.[69]

St. Gabriel's Church about 1890. St. Gabriel's Church was under construction for many years. Father Lucien Galtier, who succeeded Father Augustin Ravoux and Father Joseph Crétin as pastor of St. Gabriel's Parish, directed the completion of the church structure. The spire for the church underwent several alterations. It was removed in 1908, when the present sanctuary, two sacristies, and west entrance with two steeples were added.
(Private Collection)

1840

Rev. Augustin Ravoux and St. Gabriel's Cemetery

Mathias Loras had been consecrated as the first bishop of Dubuque at the church in Mobile, Alabama where he was living in 1837. Afterwards, he set sail for Europe to recruit priests for the newly instituted Diocese of Dubuque. While in France, he recruited two priests, Joseph Crétin and Anthony Pelamourgues, as well as four seminarians: Augustin Ravoux, Lucien Galtier, James Causse, and Remigius Petiot. They left France and made a difficult voyage of forty-five days across the Atlantic Ocean in the autumn of 1838. On their arrival in the United States, the men separated, leaving Father Pelamourgues in the seminary at Baltimore, to pursue the study of English, while his associates continued to St. Louis. There they spent the winter visiting preaching missions and performing spiritual duties. In early spring, Pelamourgues united in St. Louis with Bishop Loras and the others. They were joined by Samuel Mazzuchelli, and all took passage on the first steamboat of the season up the Mississippi River. They landed at Dubuque on April 19, 1839, amid tremendous excitement. The following Sunday, Bishop Loras was solemnly installed as bishop of the Diocese of Dubuque.

Throughout the summer and fall, the seminarians Ravoux, Galtier, Causse, and Petoit continued their studies for the priesthood. On the first of November, Bishop Loras ordained the four men as deacons. Then, on January 5, 1840, the four men were ordained priests. With a need for priests to minister to the residents of the diocese, Bishop Loras sent Father Ravoux to Prairie du Chien and Father Galtier to St. Peter's on the Minnesota River. They were not to be missionary priests but rather pastors to their parishes.

Arriving at Prairie du Chien as the first pastor of St. Gabriel's parish, Father Ravoux had a daunting task. He had to minister to the spiritual needs of his parish, find a place to live, establish records of the baptisms, marriages, and burials at which he would officiate, make the empty stone church a place for prayer, administer the sacraments, and the offer daily Mass. He took to the duties immediately. One of the first tasks he performed was the creation of a written record:

Registre
de
Catholicité
de la
Praire du Chien
1840.

In the *Registre*, Father Ravoux recorded *"Baptêmes, Mariages, Sépultures."* Finally, a permanent record had been established for the Catholic community at Prairie du Chien. The *Registre* was maintained by Father Ravoux's successors: Father Joseph Crétin and Father Lucien Galtier.[70]

Augustin Ravoux, S.J. was the first pastor of St. Gabriel's Parish in Prairie du Chien. Father Ravoux arrived at the prairie in March 1840 and then left September of the following year to minister to the Dakota. In 1843, Father Ravoux journeyed from Lac qui Parle to Dubuque for encouragement from Bishop Loras and then to Prairie du Chien for a few months. At Prairie du Chien, he resided with Father Joseph Crétin and authored *Wakantanka ti ki Chanku* (The Path to the House of God), a prayer book for the Dakota. The book was printed on a printing press belonging to Crétin, and translated from the French to Dakota by members of the Faribault family. (Private Collection)

The land that Strange Powers had given on which to build St. Gabriel's church amounted to about four acres. The church had been erected at the front of the plot, so much of the land lay behind the church structure. Father Ravoux designed a plan for a cemetery to be plotted behind the church. He platted the grounds into four quadrants, with a central west-east path and a central north-south grassy path. Two spired pillars would flank the west entrance to the cemetery.

While pastor of St. Gabriel's, Father Ravoux officiated at thirty-one burials in 1840 and sixteen in 1841. In September 1841, Father Ravoux left Prairie du Chien for Traverse des Sioux. Here, he was to minister to the Dakota living on the upper Mississippi and Minnesota Rivers. Father Joseph Crétin then became the pastor of St. Gabriel's parish. He too recorded baptisms, marriages, and burials in the *Registre*, and so did his successor, Father Lucien Galtier.

The land that Hercules L. Dousman had given to the Catholic Church in 1836 for a burying ground lay untouched for many years. Daniel Fenton, the husband of Madeline Fisher, Jane F. Dousman's niece, had been buried on the plot in 1850. By 1860, the population of Prairie du Chien had greatly increased. New arrivals from Ireland, Germany, and Bohemia were making their new homes on the prairie. The vast majority of these residents were Catholic. The space in the cemetery

This house originally stood north of St. Gabriel's Church. It was used as a chapel by Father Mazzuchelli. With the construction of St. Gabriel's Church, the structure became the parsonage. Fathers Ravoux, Crétin, and Galtier lived in the house. It was moved to its present location in the 1890s.

behind St. Gabriel's Church was limited. So, the parish erected a fence around the land located across the Highway from the Old Catholic Burying Ground to define a new cemetery. In May 1864, the land was consecrated and named Calvary Cemetery.

The Old Catholic Burying Ground had been an integral part of the community of Prairie du Chien for almost twenty-five years. By 1840, Prairie du Chien was changing. It had been a small settlement on the Mississippi River frontier whose economy was centered on the fur trade. Now, men from New York influenced the economy and immigrants from western Europe sought the availability of fertile land taken from the Native nations. Like the fur trade, the Old Catholic Burying Ground was a vestige of the past. With only a few exceptions, from April 1840 forward no deceased member of St. Gabriel's Parish was interred in the Old Catholic Burying Ground that had been blessed by Father Marie Joseph Dunand in May 1817.[71]

Bernard Walter Brisbois (1808-1885) was the son of Michel and Domitille Brisbois. B.W. helped organize the Brisbois Cemetery Association to preserve the burial sites of his parents, Michel and Domitille Brisbois. (Villa Louis State Historic Site, Wisconsin Historical Society)

1837

Brisbois Cemetery

One of the early residents of Prairie du Chien was Michel Brisbois. Michel Brisbois was born in Yamaska, Quebec about 1759. He attended school, then, like many young men, sought employment in the fur trade. An educated man, he was not a voyageur or *engage*, but operated as an independent fur trader. By 1778, he was working out of Mackinac, then settled at Prairie du Chien in 1781. His removal to the prairie coincided with the signing of a treaty.

In 1781, as the war between Great Britain and the thirteen colonies was ending, the residents of the prairie realized they needed title to the land at the prairie. They met and selected men to travel to Michilimackinac and request from the British lieutenant governor, Patrick Sinclair, title to their property. Pierre Antaya, Augustine Ange, Basile Giard, and Pierre Lapointe were the men selected. Brisbois, still residing at Mackinac, witnessed the signing of the treaty and then moved to the prairie with his family.

Brisbois continued in the fur trade, then in the early 19th century changed his occupation. Brisbois owned Main Village Lot No. 15. Here, he lived with his family, their house facing the Mississippi River. He also owned several farm lots on which, like his neighbors, he grew rye and barley. Brisbois built several ovens, hired Strange Powers as his assistant, and established himself as a baker. He baked bread for the residents of the prairie and large quantities of hard biscuits for the traders and fur companies. The biscuits, along with dried pease or corn, were a major source of sustenance during the wintering season.

Michel Brisbois had ceased to practice the Catholic faith in which he had been raised, and Father Mazzuchelli took it upon himself to bring this very important man back to the Church. During his visit to the prairie in 1835, he persistently visited Brisbois. Finally, Brisbois allowed him into his house. To the joy of his neighbors, Brisbois returned to the faith.[72]

Blind and in poor health, in 1836, Brisbois wrote his will. In it, he stated that when he died, he wished to be buried atop a bluff overlooking the prairie.[73] Michel Brisbois died in 1837.

George P. Brisbois, Michel Brisbois's son, owned half of a quarter section of land. This tract overlooked the prairie, and so the elder Brisbois was buried as he wished atop a bluff on his son's land.[74] Domitille Brisbois, Michel Brisbois's wife, died ten years later. There is no gravesite for her at the Old Catholic Burying Ground or St. Gabriel's Cemetery. Tradition holds that she was buried with her husband atop the bluff.

George Brisbois had sold the entire tract of land on which his father had been buried to his brother Bernard Walter (B. W.) in July 1841.[75] B. W. farmed the land that surround his father's and then his mother's grave. When Therese LaChapelle Brisbois, B. W.'s wife, died in 1849, she was buried within a few feet of Michel and Domitille. In tending his parents and Therese's graves, B. W. obviously gave some thought as to the future and who would care for the site after his death.

On September 8, 1866, B. W. Brisbois and seven men formed the Brisbois Cemetery Association. The other men were Ira B. Brunson, O. B. Thomas, Nicholas Smith, Lewis Stram, Joseph Tilmont, Daniel Brisbois, and F. Kappel. Ira Brunson was elected president of the association, and Smith elected the secretary. All agreed the association would meet yearly on the 8th of September. Brunson, Tilmont, and Kappel were to be the trustees of the association's assets. B. W. then sold to the Brisbois Cemetery Association, for one dollar, eighteen acres of land atop the bluff where Michel, Domitille, and Therese had been buried. Excepted from the sale of land was a lot fifty feet square stated as "only for the use of the party of the first part (B. W. Brisbois), his family relations, and friends as a burial place of the dead...." In the lot was the "grave of Michael [*sic*] Brisbois Buried in 1837." The fifty-foot square lot was surveyed, using the grave of Michel Brisbois as a marker.[76]

Brisbois Cemetery looking west towards Prairie du Chien, circa 1890. (Prairie du Chien Historical Society)

B. W. died on July 15, 1885. He had been visiting his son in Mendota, Wisconsin when he died. The Prairie du Chien *Courier* reported, "The remains were brought here and were interred in the family vault on the bluff that overlooks our beautiful Prairie City. It was the request of the deceased that the funeral should be quiet and unostentatious."[77]

The only other marked grave in the cemetery is that of Joseph Tilmont. Born in Brussels, Belgium, Tilmont settled in Prairie du Chien. He operated the Tilmont House, a hotel, and had a small enterprise that produced patent medicines. He had been one of the founders and trustee of the Brisbois Cemetery Association.[78]

A son of B. W. and Therese Brisbois may have also been buried in the cemetery. According to a newspaper account, the last person to be buried in the cemetery was a son who died in 1903. If this is so, the son was Henry, born 1846. There is no grave marker for Henry Brisbois.

Looking east from the Old Catholic Burying Ground or "Frenchtown Cemetery" across the "Highway," now County Road K, to the entrance to Calvary Cemetery. (Wisconsin Historical Society)

PART TWO

Burials Documented in Church Records, Chronological

Grand lajour

Date of Burial – 10 May 1817[1]

No information has been found to identify this person.

_____ Amiot

Date of Burial – 6 June 1817[2]

This person may have been a descendant of Jean Baptiste Amiot (circa 1720-1763). Jean Baptiste Amiot was born in Quebec. He traveled to Michilimackinac and was employed as a blacksmith. He married Marie-Anne, a Sauk woman. They had eight children, the oldest of whom was Augustin. About 1763, Jean Baptiste moved to La Baye (Green Bay).[3]

Basil Giar (Giard)

Date of Burial – 4 July 1817[4]

Born/Baptized – 25 October 1744 at Contrecoeur, Quebec[5]

Married – Makochikoue[6]/Mecoutchiquoi[7]

Soon after Father Marie Dunand left Prairie du Chien, Basile Giard died. In recording the burial, it was noted that Giard was seventy-two years old at the time of his death.

Basile Giard came to the upper Mississippi from the Kaskaskia region in southern Illinois. He traded at Prairie du Chien as early as 1779. In 1781, Giard was one of the men representing all the residents of Prairie du Chien, and who was present for the signing of a treaty at Michilimackinac. Lt. Governor Patrick Sinclair negotiated a treaty with representatives of the Native nations in which the leaders gave land at Michilimackinac, Green Bay, and Prairie du Chien to the residents of the communities. The three men, Giard, Pierre Antaya, and Augustin Ange, then returned to Prairie du Chien and distributed goods to the Native nations in payment for the prairie.[8]

In his testimony, Giard stated he moved from Prairie du Chien to the west bank of the Mississippi about 1785. Here, he built a home and farmed. He had no title to the land, so on October 15, 1800, he petitioned the Spanish governor at St. Louis to grant him title to an area of 6,808½ arpents. Giard lived on his tract with his wife, Mecoutchiquoi, and three daughters. Their children were Louise, Angelique, and Marie. He still maintained a connection with Prairie du Chien. The prairie became part of Indiana Territory in 1800, and when the militia of St. Clair County was formed two years later, Giard was appointed a lieutenant in the Seventh Company.[9]

Though his property on the west side of the Mississippi River was surveyed in 1807, Giard never received title to his land, which was now part of the Louisiana territory controlled by the United States. He therefore abandoned it. In 1808, Giard moved his family to Lot No. 21 in the Main Village of Prairie du Chien. Giard had occupied this lot as early as 1788. Here, he had built a house.[10]

In 1817, Giard sold his lot in the Main Village, which included a house and dependencies, to Joseph Rolette; but Giard remained in the house until the time of his death.[11] (See Angelique Giard Lupien and Marie Giard Bell.)

Catherine Antaya

Date of Burial – 10 October 1817[12]

Baptized – 2 May 1817, at Prairie du Chien[13]

On May 2, 1817, Father Dunand recorded that he had baptized Catherine. She was twenty years of age and the daughter of Pierre Antaya and a Fox woman.[14]

Josette Antaya

Date of Burial – 22 November 1818[15]

Married – 8 May 1817 Charles Lapointe, at Prairie du Chien[16]

With the burial record, someone noted that Josette was the wife of Charles Lapointe. Father Dunand had married the couple the previous year. He recorded that Charles Lapointe was the son of François Lapointe and Rosalie Miron, a native of Quebec, and Josette was the daughter of Pierre Peltier *dit* Antaya and a Fox woman. After blessing the couple's marriage, Dunand then baptized their daughter, Suzanne, who had been born March 20, 1816.[17] Prior to her marriage to Charles Lapointe, Josette lived with Julien Dubuque. In testimony concerning Dubuque's estate, Josette stated that she served Dubuque and his family as housekeeper. Dubuque died in 1810.[18]

Joseph Duplese

Date of Burial – 20 June 1819[19]

Born – circa 1778

The date of Joseph Duplese's burial occurred after Father Dunand had left Prairie du Chien. Father Dunand had left the Register, or a copy of the Register, with one of the residents of Prairie du Chien. The person who maintained the Register, or someone, noted in the Register that at the time of Duplese's death, he believed the age of Duplese to be forty-one years.[20]

In July 1816, Duplese had signed an engagement to work for Jean Baptiste Bertholet at Prairie du Chien.[21] Duplese also signed the petition sent to the United States Congress in 1816 by the residents of Prairie du Chien requesting confirmation of ownership of their land on the prairie.[22]

Josefe Marie Mercier

Date of Burial – 7 December 1819[23]

Born – circa 1807

Baptized – 12 May 1817, at Prairie du Chien

Father Dunand had baptized Joseph Mercier during his visit to Prairie du Chien, noting the boy was ten years of age and the son of Felix Mercier and Louise Giar (Giard).[24]

Pier Lessar (Pierre Lessard)

Date of Burial – 1 February 1823[25]

Born – 24 August 1810, at Prairie du Chien[26]

Baptized – 23 April 1817, at Prairie du Chien[27]

Pierre was the son of Pierre Lessard and Julie Crely. This can be determined by two entries in the records maintained by Father François Vincent Badin. After the death of young Pierre, Pierre Lessard and Julie Crely Lessard had another son, Jean Baptiste, who was born October 4, 1825. Pierre and Julie were also present at the burial of another son on May 18, 1829.[28] (See following entry for [Male] Lessart.)

Victoire Bizanne (Pizanne)

Date of Burial – 19 April 1823[29]

Baptized – 8 May 1817, sixteen years of age, at Prairie du Chien[30]

Victoire was the daughter of Pierre Lapointe and a Sioux woman. According to Therese Lapointe Barrette, Victoire married Edward Pizanne.[31]

J. Batiste Cardinal

Date of Burial – 20 April 1823[32]

Though written as J. Batiste Cardinal, this may have been Jean Marie Cardinal. Jean Marie had married Elizabeth Antaya. After his death, a marriage contract was executed on January 17, 1824, between Jean Baptist Ouillette and Elizabeth Antaille "veuve de Jean Marie Cardinal" (widow of Jean Marie Cardinal). The contract contained an inventory of Elizabeth's possessions that included a piece of land three arpents wide, a house and furnishings, and cash.[33] Eight years later, Jean Baptiste Wellette (Ouillette) sold a piece of land in the Village of St. Friole, "known by the name of Jean Marie Cardinal's Lot," to Abraham Trepagnier. This lot was "3 arpents in front...."[34]

_____ Trepanier

Date of Burial – 25 August 1823[35]

This was probably a child of Abraham Trepanniée and Amelia Drew. Abraham was from the parish of Riviere du Loups, Quebec. In 1817, he signed an engagement to work for the partnership of Jean Baptiste Bertholet and Joseph Rolette and to spend two winters in the dependencies of Michilimackinac.[36] Abraham and Amelia had a daughter Julia, born about 1840.[37]

Pier Gauselin (Pierre Gosselin)

Date of Burial – 23 January 1824[38]

Died – 22 January 1824[39]

According to probate records, Pierre died intestate at Prairie du Chien. His name was recorded as Pierre Gosselin.[40]

Gosselin was a voyageur finding employment with various fur trade companies and independent traders that operated out of Mackinac and Prairie du Chien. In 1808, Gosselin signed an engagement to work for the Mackinac Company among the Sauk. In 1809, the Company employed him to work at Prairie du Chien. As the fur trade reorganized after the War of 1812, Gosselin helped transport goods from Mackinac to Prairie du Chien for the trading company of Rolette and Bertholet for the trading year of 1815. The following year, Joseph St. John hired him to winter on the Mississippi.[41]

Gosselin was one of the "Canadian Voyageurs" who was listed on June 21, 1814, who had volunteered their service at Mackinac to go to Prairie du Chien. Gosselin was part of a combined force of volunteers and Native men who traveled from Michilimackinac to Prairie du Chien, whose purpose was to attack the American fort built on the prairie.[42]

From 1817 to 1821, Gosselin was in the employment of the American Fur Company. In 1817, he signed an engagement to be a boatman for Russell Farnham, an agent of the American Fur Company, who traded in the Fond du Lac Department. Gosselin then worked in the Lac du Flambeau department of the American Fur Company for several seasons.[43]

Gosselin probably retired from the fur trade and lived at Prairie du Chien. His estate included an extensive wardrobe, which was sold at auction. The items were purchased by other voyageurs.[44]

Marianne Souligne, Dame Colas

Date of Burial – 30 March 1824[45]

In the 1816 petition from the residents of Prairie du Chien to the U.S. Congress, Marianne Souligne signed as Veuve (widow) Colas.[46]

Marianne Souligne had probably been born in Canada. She had lived at St. Joseph (Michigan) and then migrated to the Illinois Country. At Cahokia, she married Jean Marie Cardinal, who was trading at Prairie du Chien in the 1780s. Cardinal and Marie Souligne moved to Prairie du Chien, residing on the prairie by 1794. They built a small house on Farm Lot No. 15, and then in 1799, Souligne had a larger house constructed on the lot. When Cardinal died, Souligne married Nicholas Colas. Cardinal had claimed several farm lots on the prairie, which passed to Souligne. By 1824, she had sold most of her land to Joseph Rolette.[47]

Joseph Crelie (often spelled Crely) was born at Kaskaskia in 1773 and moved to Prairie du Chien about 1792. He died at Portage on January 27, 1866. (Wisconsin Historical Society)

B. W. Brisbois related a story about Marianne Souligne. "After Cardinal's death, [Marianne] married her servant man Colas, who was very nearly white; and for her third husband, Joseph Crélie — but that after a three days' blissful matrimonial experience with the latter, she was yet vigorous enough to kick him out of bed and drive him off. This latter marriage must have been somewhere about 1820, when Crélie did not exceed fifty and would hardly have been smitten with the charms of a lady who had enjoyed the suns of over one hundred and twenty summers."[48]

Augustin Mason

Date of Burial – 23 October 1824[49]

According to Michel Brisbois, as early as 1794 Mason had claimed the right of cutting hay on Farm Lot No. 29 and four years later enclosed and occupied the land.[50]

Victoire Urtubise (Hurtibise/Hurtibus)

Date of Burial – 17 March 1825[51]

Married – 8 September 1817 John Findley, at Prairie du Chien[52]

Victoire Hurtibise, the daughter of Jean Baptiste Hurtibise, and John Findley were married by the Rev. Samuel Peters, "as they were of lawful age and had the consent of their parents."[53]

Victoire wrote her last will and testament on March 8, 1825. She bequeathed her featherbed, clothing, and kitchen tools to Archange Barrette, her cousin, who had taken care of her in her sickness. Joseph Rolette was made guardian of her two sons (not named).[54]

John Findley and Joseph Barrette, the husband of Archange, had been killed a few years before at the mouth of the Chippewa River. The men had met a party of Ojibwe. An altercation ensued, and Findley and Barrette were killed.[55]

Victoire was the half-sister of Marguerite DuBois, the first wife of Joseph Rolette.[56] (See Marguerite DuBois.)

Michel Periar (Perillard)

Date of Burial – 1825[57]

Married – 1 June 1825 Marie Mercier, at Prairie du Chien[58]

Michel was born in Quebec and lived in the parish of Ste-Geneviève. In 1815, he signed an engagement to work for the North West Company as a "Gouvernail dans un de leur Canots ou Bateaux" (person to maintain the rudder in one of the canoes or bateaux) who would be traveling to Prairie du Chien.[59]

On April 22, 1817, Father Dunand baptized Ale[x]andre, the son of Michel Periard and Marie Mercier.[60] "Michael [sic] Perillard" and "Mary [sic] Mercier" were married in June 1825 in a civil ceremony by J. H. Lockwood, JP.[61]

Michel died shortly after his marriage. On May 5, 1825, he sold property in "that part of Prairie du Chien called Saint Freole..." to James Lockwood. After his death, Marie Mercier settled Michel's estate and sold Lot No. 4 in the Main Village to H. L. Dousman for $25.00.[62]

Angelle Rolette

Date of Burial – 20 September 1825[63]

Born – 17 September 1791 in Quebec[64]

Angele-Elizabeth was the daughter of Jean Joseph Rolette (1744-1828) and Marie Angelique Lortie. She was the sister of Jean Joseph Rolette, the Prairie du Chien fur trader.[65]

François Regis Gagne (Gagnier)

Date of Burial – 29 June 1827[66]

Baptized – 13 May 1817, twenty-one years of age, at Prairie du Chien[67]

Married – 24 November 1823 Therese Chalifoux, at Prairie du Chien[68]

Died – 28 June 1827

Father Badin recorded that Gagne "30 years of age, killed by the Indians yesterday at noon, was buried by us the undersigned priest, June 29, 1827, in the presence of John Simpson and Augustin Hebert, who were not able to sign as required."[69]

François Regis was the son of Claude Gagnier and Marianne Labuche.[70] François and Therese had two children: François, born December 6, 1824, and baptized June 9, 1827; and Marie Regis, born August 15, 1826, and baptized June 21, 1827.[71]

Marie Louise Gagnier was the daughter of François Regis Gagnier and Therese Chalifoux. She was born August 15, 1826 and survived the attack that killed her father. She married Amable Moreaux August 11, 1843. Father Joseph Crétin blessed the marriage on August 25. After Moreaux's death, Marie Louise married Cosmo Cherrier on March 1, 1862. She died February 10, 1893. (Prairie du Chien Historical Society)

Denis Courtois

Date of Burial – 18 July 1827[72]

Born – circa 1799

Died – 17 July 1827

Father Badin recorded that Denis Courtois "...age 28, died yesterday at 8:30 P. M. and was buried in the parish cemetery in the presence of his father."[73] The parents of Denis Courtois were Denis Courtois and Marie Blondo (Blondeau).

Marie Blondeau Courtois was not present at her son's burial. She must have been sick as she died the same day Denis was buried. (See the following entry.)

Marie Blondeau

Date of Burial – 19 July 1827[74]

Born – circa 1769

Married – 29 April 1817 Denis Courtois, at Prairie du Chien[75]

Died – 18 July 1827

Father Badin recorded "...wife of Denis Courtois, about 58 years of age, died yesterday at 9 P. M. and was buried in the parish cemetery in the presence of her husband."[76]

The first marriage performed at Prairie du Chien by Father Dunand was the joining of Denis Courtois and Marie Blondeau. Dunand recorded that Denis was the son of Charles Courtois and Catherine St. Cosmo. Denis was a native of Detroit residing at Prairie du Chien. Marie was the legitimate daughter of Drezi Blondo and Genevieve Legnio and a native of Quebec, also residing at Prairie du Chien.[77]

In 1820, Denis Courtois, the father, was one of the three men who had lived at Prairie du Chien for the longest time. Isaac Lee relied upon Courtois' testimony to prove that the Indian claim to the prairie had been extinguished. In his testimony for Lee, Courtois stated he was fifty-two years old and had been a resident of Prairie du Chien for twenty-nine years (1791). Courtois' testimony helped many who lived on the north end of the prairie gain title to their land. Courtois claimed ownership of Farm Lot No. 8.[78] In the early 19th century, the open backwater across from his farm was called Courtois' Pond.

Denis, the father, died in 1843 leaving four living daughters: Celest Cherrier, Elisabeth Grimard, Felicite McNair, and Madelaine Anderson. The north half of Farm Lot No. 8 was divided among the four girls and the heirs of Charles Courtois and Teotice Pion, deceased.[79] With the passing of Denis and a portion of Denis' property now owned by Pierre and Elisabeth Grimard, the name of the pond changed to Gremore Lake, Gremore the anglicization of Grimard.

Jean Baptiste Wemet (Ouimette)

Date of Burial – 20 November 1828

Born – circa 1772

Died – 18 November 1828[80]

Father Badin recorded Wemet "56 years of age, died the day before yesterday, and was buried in the parish cemetery in the presence of François Chenever[t], Joseph Rivard, and many others."[81]

The burial recorded is that of Jean Baptiste Wemette, Sr. He lived with his son, Jean Baptiste Wemette, Jr. in the Middle Village, or Village of St. Friole Lot No. 17, on which there was a house, a barn, and a stable. Prior to his father's death, Wemette, Jr. had fallen ill and never recovered. He later died July 17, 1829. The two estates were joined, and their property and belongings sold at auction under the administration of Joseph Brisbois.[82] The burial of Jean Baptiste Wemette, Jr. was not recorded in Father Badin's register, as he died after Father Badin left the prairie.

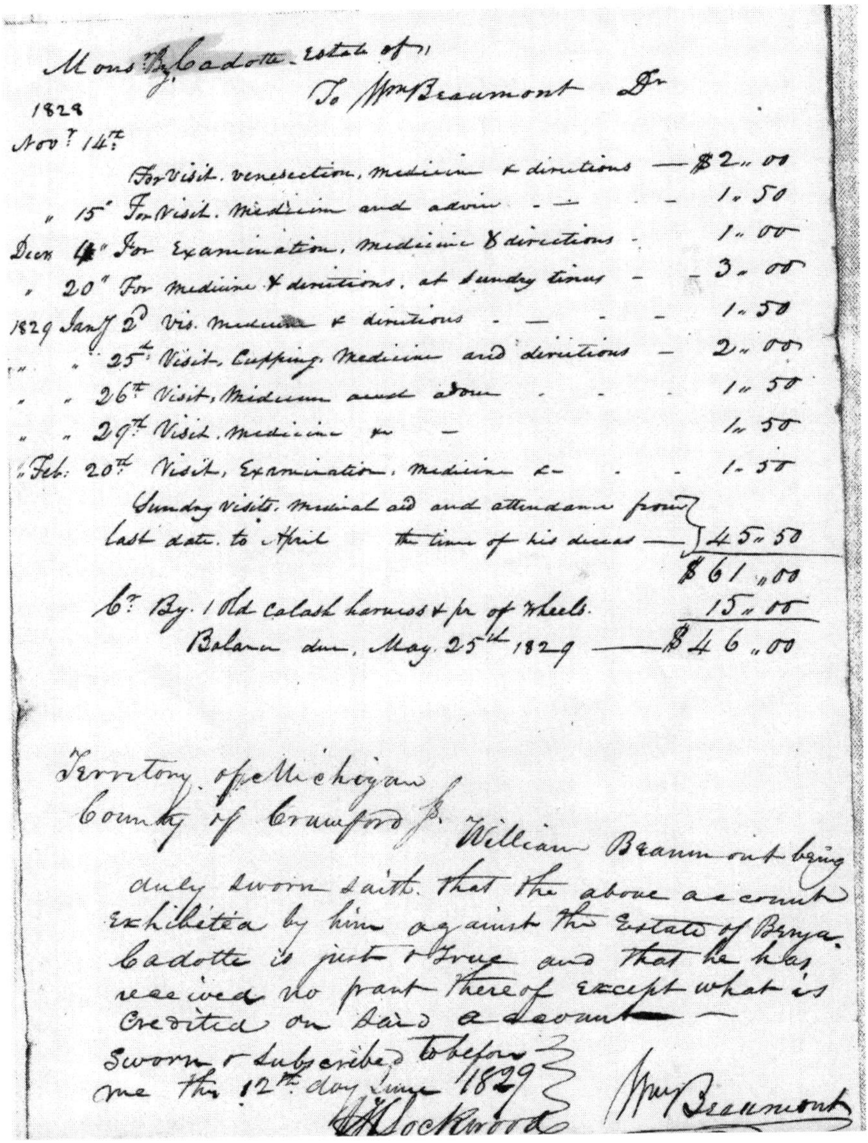

Mons. B. Cadotte estate of
To Wm Beaumont Dr

1828
Novr 14th For Visit, venesection, medicine & directions — $2.00
" 15th For Visit. Medicine and advice — 1.50
Decr 4th For Examination, medicine & directions — 1.00
" 20th For medicine & directions, at sundry times — 3.00
1829 Jany 2d Vis. medicine & directions — 1.50
" 25th Visit, Cupping, Medicine and directions — 2.00
" 26th Visit, Medicine and advice — 1.50
" 29th Visit, medicine &c — 1.50
" Feb. 20th Visit, Examination, medicine &c — 1.50
Sundry visits, medical aid and attendance from last date to April the time of his decease — 45.50
$61.00
Cr By 1 old calash harness & pr of wheels 15.00
Balance due, May 25th 1829 — $46.00

Territory of Michigan
County of Crawford ss.
William Beaumont being duly sworn saith that the above account exhibited by him against the Estate of Benja. Cadotte is just & true and that he has received no part thereof except what is credited on said account —
Sworn & subscribed to before me this 12th day June 1829
J. H. Lockwood
Wm Beaumont

Bill from Dr. William Beaumont for his care of Benjamin Cadotte from November 14, 1828 to "the time of his decease."

The assumption may be made that Jean Baptiste Wemette, Jr. was also buried in this cemetery.

William Beaumont was the U.S. Army surgeon stationed at Fort Crawford at the time of the father and son's illnesses. Beaumont cared for Jean Baptiste father and son from October 1828 through July 17, 1829. Jean Baptiste, the son, was so ill that Beaumont cared for him in the post hospital from January 24 to March 7, 1829.[83] (See Jean Baptiste Wemet, Jr.)

Augustin (Courville)

Date of Burial – 1 December 1828

Born – 30 November 1828, at Prairie du Chien

Baptized – 30 November 1828, at Prairie du Chien[84]

Died – 30 November 1828

Father Badin recorded the burial of Augustin "...who died yesterday, the son of an unknown father and Louise Courville in the presence of Charles Menard and Michel Mercier."[85] Father Badin had baptized the boy the day he was born, with Joseph Rivard standing as godfather and Marguerite Leblanc as godmother.[86]

Augustin Hebert *dit* Lablanc

Date of Burial – 2 December 1828

Born – circa 1777, in Quebec

Married (?) – Cheenaeapauky,[87] a Fox woman[88]

Died – 30 November 1828[89]

Father Badin recorded that Hebert was "51 years of age, died the day before yesterday and was buried in the parish cemetery."[90]

Hebert was from the parish of St. François in Quebec. In 1819, he signed an engagement to work as a voyageur traveling to Michilimackinac.[91]

Hebert, by his own testimony, acquired land at Prairie du Chien as early as 1805. Four years later, he enclosed and occupied Farm Lot No. 22. At some date he also acquired Farm Lots Nos. 16 and 17 and a lot in the Upper Village. He provided testimony for claims on other farm lots as to their use since the 1790s. It is hard to determine whether he had been at Prairie du Chien since that time.[92] He did sign the petition in 1816 requesting title to his property.[93]

Hebert was employed as a boatman in the Lac du Flambeau Department of the American Fur Company, as part of the outfits organized from 1819 through 1822.[94]

On May 7, 1817, Father Dunand baptized four daughters of Augustin Hebert and a "Fox woman." They were: Louise, seven years of age; Françoise, four years of age; Marie Anne, three years of age; and Marguerite, two years of age.[95]

Upon Hebert's death, Charles Menard, Jr. presented Hebert's will to the court, which Hebert had written the day before his death. In the will, Hebert named Menard's wife, Françoise Hebert, and one of her sisters (not named) as heirs. At his death, Hebert owned Farm Lot No. 22 with a house and a barn, which he had enclosed and occupied since 1809, and the village lot that lay across the road, which he had owned since 1805.[96]

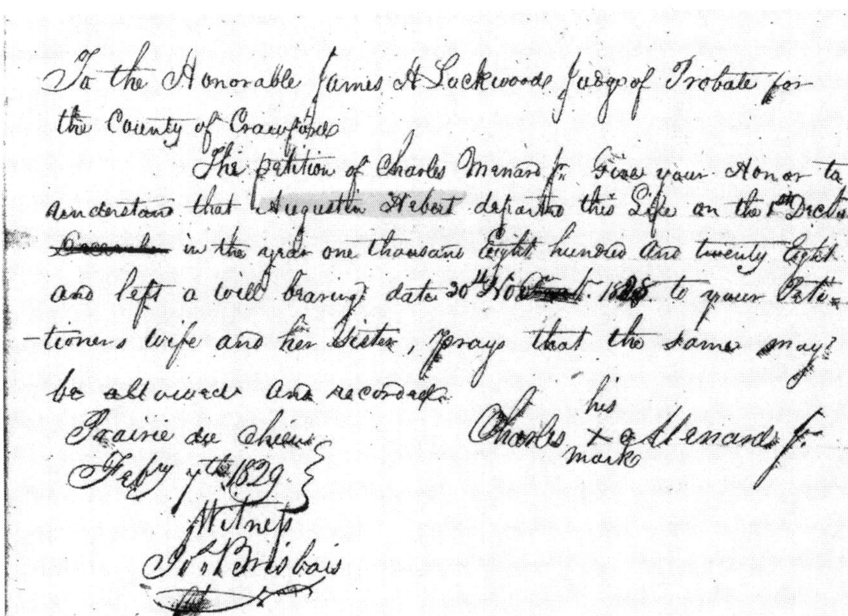
To the Honorable James H Lockwood Judge of Probate for
the County of Crawford
The petition of Charles Menard Jr. Gives your Honor to
understand that Augustin Hebert departed this Life on the 1st Decbr
~~December~~ in the year one thousand Eight hundred and twenty Eight
and left a will bearing date 30th November 1828. to your Peti-
-tioners wife and her Sister, prays that the same may
be allowed and recorded.
Prairie du Chien
Feby 7th 1829
his
Charles x Menard Jr.
mark
Witness
J. Brisbois

Petition of Charles Menard, Jr. requesting the will of Augustin Hebert be entered into probate. February 7, 1829.

Archange _____

Date of Burial – 4 March 1829

Born – circa 1789

Died – 3 March 1829[97]

Father Badin recorded that Archange "...about 40 years of age, died yesterday and was buried in the parish cemetery in the presence of Francois Chenever, Charles Menard, and many others."[98] Archange's last name has not been identified.

Benjamin Cadotte

Date of Burial – 18 April 1829

Born – circa 1779

Married – 2 May 1816 Josette Ange, at Prairie du Chien[99]

(See Josette Ange Cadotte.)

Died – 16 April 1829[100]

Benjamin Cadotte and Josette Ange had a son Henry, born January 29, 1817, and baptized April 23, 1817.[101]

Father Badin recorded that Cadotte "...about 50 years of age, died April 16, 1829 and was buried in the parish cemetery in the presence of Charles Menard, Pierre Lessart and many others."[102]

In 1807, Cadotte was a voyageur engaged to work for François Frenière on the Mississippi. In 1808, he worked on the St. Peters (Minnesota) River for the Mackinac Company, then in 1809 he wintered on the Mississippi. In 1810, he worked for Michel Cadotte among the Folie Avoine (Ojibwe).[103]

About 1810, Cadotte settled at Prairie du Chien. He purchased Farm Lot. No 11 from Joseph Rolette and a lot in the Upper Village from Marie Levigne. He gave testimony to support the claims on Farm Lots Nos. 18 and 19.[104] Cadotte continued to live at Prairie du Chien and in 1816 married Josette Ange. He signed the petition in 1816 requesting title to his property. For the 1818-1819 fur trade season, he worked for the American Fur Company as a boatman.[105]

Cadotte became ill November 1828 and was attended by Dr. William Beaumont until his death in April 1829. According to the petition presented to the court, Cadotte died without a will, leaving no widow. Michel Brisbois and Oliver Cherrier made an inventory and appraisal of Cadotte's estate. He owned a farm and a village lot with a house. Judging by the inventory, the house was well-furnished, and Cadotte owned a chest of carpentry tools and extensive farm equipment. Rolette stated that he, as representative of the American Fur Company, was the principle creditor against the estate. Rolette requested the court's permission to sell Cadotte's house, farm, and personal property at auction. The proceeds of the auction covered Cadotte's debts to the American Fur Company to the penny.[106]

Jozette Crely (Josephine)

Date of Burial – 5 May 1829

Born – circa 1807

Baptized – 28 April 1817, at Prairie du Chien[107]

Married – 18 January 1823 Pierre Legris, at Prairie du Chien[108]

Died – 4 May 1829[109]

Josephine Crely was the daughter of Joseph Crelie/Crely and Françoise Antaya. (See entry for Françoise Antaya Crely Courville.) Father Badin recorded "...wife of Pierre Legris, 22 years of age, died yesterday and was buried in the parish cemetery in the presence of Charles Menard, Pierre Lessart and many others."[110] Pierre and Jozette's daughter, Sophie, had been born April 18, 1829, and baptized six days later. Only Pierre was present for his daughter's baptism.[111]

(Male) Lessart

Date of Burial – 18 May 1829

Born – circa 1823, at Prairie du Chien

Died – 17 May 1829[112]

Father Badin recorded "A child, 6 years old, of Pierre Lessard and Julie Crely, died yesterday and was buried in the parish cemetery in the presence of his father and mother, of François Chenever[t] and many others."[113] This child was probably Ignace Lessard born February 22, 1822, and baptized August 6, 1827.[114] (See entry for Julie Crely.)

Josette Crochiere

Date of Burial – 9 August 1852

Born – circa 1788

Married – 12 May 1817 John Simpson, at Prairie du Chien[115]

Married – 28 September 1835 Alexis Crochiere, at Prairie du Chien[116]

Died – 8 August 1852

Father Lucien Galtier recorded the death of Josette Crochiere in *Baptêmes, Mariages, Sépultures*, the register for St. Gabriel's parish, begun in 1840 by Father Augustin Ravoux and maintained by the pastors of St. Gabriel's church. Father Galtier wrote, "In the year of our Lord J.C. 1852 and on the 9th of August I the undersigned C. priest certify that I have given the ecl. Scriptures to the remains of Josette Crochier who died yesterday, aged sixty-four years, she was buried in the old C. grave yard, upon her expressed desire before dying."[117]

Josette Simpson had married Alexis Crochiere in a civil ceremony performed by H. L. Dousman, J. P.[118]

According to Therese Lapoint Barrette, Josette was the daughter of Michel Antaya and Marie Menard. Josette had married John "Sandy" Simpson. Upon his death, she married Alexis Crochiere, a native of Montreal. This is confirmed in the records maintained by Father Dunand. John "Sandy" Simpson was the son of John Simpson and Marie Makintuch (MacIntosh) of Canada, and Josephine "Josette" was the daughter of Michel Peltier and Marie Menard of Cahokia (Illinois).[119]

Josette resided on Upper Village Lot No. 12 that had been granted to John Simpson. On October 13, 1851, she deeded this lot to Alexis Crochiere and his heirs.[120]

In 1814, Alexis Crochiere resided at The Bay (Green Bay). He volunteered to be a member of the expedition traveling to Prairie du Chien to attack the fort constructed by the United States.[121]

Burials Documented by Grave Markers, Chronological

Virginia Rolette

Born – 6 January 1823/1824

Died – 13 October 1839

Virginia Rolette was the daughter of Jean Joseph and Jane Fisher Rolette. Joseph Rolette wanted all of his children to receive a good education. When Virginia was about the age of thirteen, Rolette placed her in the care of Ramsey Crooks, director of the American Fur Company, and she traveled to New York to complete her education. Crooks first placed her in a private school in Flushing, New York. Then in 1837, she was enrolled in the Academy of the Visitation in Georgetown, Virginia. She remained at the school for two years. During that time, her brother Joseph Rolette, who was in New York completing his education, visited Virginia, as did her half-sister, Elizabeth. In October 1839, Rolette withdrew Virginia from the Academy, and she began her trip to return to Prairie du Chien. Virginia had not been well, and she became ill while on the steamboat traveling up the Mississippi to Prairie du Chien. About eighty miles from home, Virginia died of "cerebral congestion."[122]

After the Dousman family plot was established in Calvary Cemetery, the remains of Virginia Rolette were disinterred and reburied in the Dousman plot. Land for what became Calvary Cemetery was donated by Hercules L. Dousman to the Catholic Church in 1836. The "new Catholic Cemetery," as it was called, was not consecrated until May 1864.[123] The reburial of Virginia Rolette would not have occurred until after 1864 or perhaps not until after the death and burial of her mother, Jane Fisher Rolette Dousman. Jane died January 13, 1882.

Two unknown women visit the Old Catholic Burying Ground or "Frenchtown Cemetery" and gaze at the graves of Joseph Rolette and Elizabeth Rolette. (Wisconsin Historical Society)

Joseph Rolette

Born – 23 September 1781[124]

Married – 10 February 1817 Marguerite DuBois[125]

Married – 29 January 1818 Genevieve (Jane) Fisher[126]

Died – 3 December 1842

Jean Joseph Rolette, the son of Jean Joseph and Marie Angelique Lortie Rolette, was born in Quebec, the third of fifteen children. He was a student at the Seminaire de Quebec from 1792 to 1799. He left Quebec for Montreal and worked for Dominique Lecroix. From there Rolette traveled to Detroit and Sandwich, where he met Murdoch Cameron. Cameron traded on the Mississippi River above Prairie du Chien, and Rolette went to work for Cameron, who placed Rolette at Lac-qui-Parle on the St. Peters/Minnesota River.[127]

Rolette formed a relationship with Marguerite (also listed as Margaret) DuBois, whose mother was a relative of the Dakota leader, Wapasha. On August 9, 1811, Joseph sold to Margaret for "$1 and love and affection" a piece of land at Prairie du Chien. Included in the sale were livestock and "one single stove together with all the household furniture and kitchen utensils." So, there must have been a house on the property.[128] The sale occurred one month before the birth of their first daughter, Emilie. From this union, Rolette and Marguerite had three daughters: Emilie, born September 11, 1811; Elizabeth, born November 7, 1813; and Henriette, born "December 19, 1813 [sic]." They were baptized on April 23, 1817, by Father Dunand, who noted that Joseph and Marguerite had a civil marriage.[129] Joseph and Marguerite Rolette had been married on February 10, 1817, by Nicholas Boilvin, Justice of the Peace.[130] The assumption is that Marguerite died in 1817. The property that Joseph had given her was acquired by James Aird in 1818.[131]

On January 29, 1818, Rolette married Genevieve Fisher.[132] They moved into a house in the Main Village south of the Brisbois family on the lot Rolette had purchased from Basile Giard in 1818.[133] Genevieve, who became known as Jane, was the daughter of Henry Munro Fisher. Fisher had left Prairie du Chien in 1814, placing Jane and her brother George with Michel and Domitille Brisbois. Joseph Rolette and Jane Fisher's marriage united the old fur trade with the new. In 1816, when the United States Army arrived in Prairie du Chien, both Michel Brisbois and Joseph Rolette were feared as the most influential men in the community. Rolette was banished to an island in the Mississippi River, and Brisbois was transported to St. Louis.[134]

Two children are documented as born to Joseph and Jane Rolette: Joseph, born 1820; and Virginia, born 1823/1824. There are no records of their births or baptisms. The birth dates are those inscribed on their tombstones.

By 1820, Rolette had risen to be the most important and wealthiest man in the village. Prairie du Chien was the center for the fur trade on the upper Mississippi. All trade goods were transported by water to the traders at Prairie du Chien then dispersed north and west to various trading sites along the tributaries of the Mississippi River. In the spring, the furs came to Prairie du Chien for transshipment to Mackinac, then onto Montreal and New York. Rolette gained control of much of the Dakota trade on the Mississippi and Minnesota Rivers.

Recognizing his influence and his control of the upper Mississippi trade, the American Fur Company entered into an agreement with Joseph Rolette in 1821. By this agreement, Rolette remained an independent trader, able to set his own price for buying furs. Rolette in turn agreed to purchase all his trade goods through the American Fur Company and then sell to the Company all the furs he had received in trade. Rolette directed the Upper Mississippi Outfit, with numerous voyageurs in his employ. Under Rolette, the American Fur Company was able to fiercely compete against the Columbia Fur Company for a monopoly of the trade in Minnesota. The competition was so harsh and consuming that Rolette had a hard time keeping the Company's business affairs in order. Ramsey Crooks decided to send Hercules L. Dousman to Prairie du Chien. Dousman was a clerk for the American Fur Company at Mackinac, and he arrived at Prairie du Chien in 1826 to work in the same capacity.

In 1834, John Jacob Astor retired, and the American Fur Company was reorganized under Ramsey Crooks. Rolette's Upper Mississippi Outfit became the Western Outfit. Rolette, Dousman, and Henry Sibley of Mendota (Minnesota) were partners on a percentage basis. Rolette remained the senior partner, with fifty percent interest. The following year, Rolette purchased a piece of land in the Main Village from Michel Brisbois. Located on the waterfront across from the steamboat landing, it was a prime piece of real estate. Rolette had a two-and-a-half-story stone warehouse erected. Calling it "Rolette's Stone Store," Rolette leased the structure to the American Fur Company.

Rolette was involved in other economic ventures. In 1829, Joseph Rolette and James Lockwood, who had come to Prairie du Chien in 1816 and had originally worked as a clerk for the American Fur Company, established a sawmill on the Chippewa River.

In the late 1830s, Rolette's position in Prairie du Chien began to decline. He had begun to drink, and his marriage was falling apart. When Rolette and Jane Fisher had married, she was a young woman with little education. When she became the mother of two children, Rolette saw to her education, filled their home with furnishing from St. Louis, and sent her and the children to Cincinnati. Their son Joseph, after his education in New York, moved to Mendota (Minnesota), working with Henry Sibley to learn the fur trade; Virginia was sent to a Catholic school in Georgetown. With no children at home, the couple grew apart. In 1836, Jane filed for separation from Rolette, and articles of separation were drawn on September 22, 1836. In them, Joseph agreed to keep Jane "in a manner suitable to her condition." Through B. W. Brisbois, Jane's cousin, Rolette agreed to pay Jane $300.00 year, plus supply all the food stuffs she might need, ranging from 500 pounds of beef to a half a pound of nutmeg. Rolette also agreed to provide her with a servant and to build for her a "stone dwelling house."[134] Now, more and more, Dousman and Sibley were making the decisions in regard to the fur trade. In 1840, the Western Outfit's contract was renewed with American Fur, and all three men became equal partners. Rolette's daughter Elizabeth attended him. Though he drank and smoked heavily, he was still found to be vivacious and good tempered. He enjoyed visitors and would regale them with stories late into the night.

The Western Outfit did not do well. Many of the Native nations on the upper Mississippi had signed treaties with the United States government, relinquishing their lands and had been moved to reservations. Rolette was also in poor health and poor financial shape. He was so badly in debt that he could not maintain his annual support of Jane. He was forced to mortgage his Stone Store property, with B. W. Brisbois holding the note. By the end of 1842, the American Fur Company was bankrupt. Dousman and Sibley signed an agreement to do business through Pierre Chouteau, Jr. and Company, headquartered in St. Louis, Missouri. Rolette was involved in the agreement but was to have no "voice or control in the business." Rolette was sick and died several months later. By 1838, Lockwood was no longer involved in the sawmills. Dousman owned half interest in the mill, with Rolette and Sibley each having a quarter share. According to the account books for the mill, Rolette was also in debt to the mills when he died.

Joseph Rolette signed his will on June 3, 1842. He left his property at Prairie du Chien to his son Joseph, his daughters Elizabeth and Emilie, and his "Natural son" Michael. He appointed Joseph and Emilie executors.[136] After Rolette died, Hercules L. Dousman took Emilie to court, arguing that he should be administrator of Rolette's estate. Dousman gained letters of administration. The debts from the Western Outfit and the sawmill were charged against Rolette and depleted his estate. Emilie fought the accounting presented by Dousman for many years but was unsuccessful in even retaining the Rolette family home.[137]

Headstone of Jean Joseph Rolette as it looks today. (Wisconsin Historical Society)

Elizabeth Rolette

Date of Burial – 9 May 1843

Born – 7 November 1813[138]

Baptized – 23 April 1817[139]

Died – 7 May 1843[140]

Father Crétin recorded in *Baptêmes, Mariages, Sépultures* "Elizabeth Rollette [sic] died day before yesterday age 28."[141]

Elizabeth was the second of three girls born to Joseph Rolette and Marguerite DuBois.[142] She lived her entire life in Prairie du Chien, taking care of her father after his separation from Jane. She was named the administrator of her father's estate but was too ill to fulfill the responsibilities, and so, Rolette amended his will to appoint Emilie Rolette Hooe, his eldest daughter, and his only son, Joseph, as administrators.[143] Elizabeth died five months after Joseph's death.

Less than two weeks before Joseph's death, Elizabeth executed her will, leaving any inheritance from her father and "benefit all my personal estate of every description of which I may possess at the time of my death" to her sister Emilie.[144]

Mrs. Alexander Gardipie

Died – on about 19 July 1840[145]

Father Ravoux recorded in Baptisms, Marriages and Burials that on July 19, 1840, he had given "Madame Gardipie" an ecclesiastical burial. While Father Ravoux did not record as to where Mrs. Gardepie was buried, early photographs of the Old Catholic Burying Grounds document that she was buried in this graveyard.

The grave of Mrs. Alexander Gardepie was marked with a wood cross and surrounded by a picket fence. Bills and receipts from the 1820s and 1830s document that various graves in the Old Catholic Burying Ground were marked with a fence. (Wisconsin Historical Society)

Mary Gaffney

Died – 1860

Alice Trewe

Died – January 1862

The inscription on the headstone states that Alice was the daughter of Ira Shoemaker.

Headstone of Alice Trewe as it looks today.

People Who Died at Prairie du Chien, 1816-1840, and May Be Buried in the Old Catholic Burying Ground, Alphabetical

Josette Ange Cadotte

Married – 2 May 1816 Benjamin Cadotte, at Prairie du Chien[146]

Died – before April 1829

Benjamin Cadotte had married Josette Ange on May 2, 1816. Josette was identified as the daughter of Augustin Ange.[147] At the time of the death of Benjamin Cadotte, Joseph Rolette testified that Cadotte had died without a will, leaving no widow. It therefore can be assumed that Josette died prior to April 1829, and that in all probability was buried in the "old C. burying grounds."[148] (See Benjamin Cadotte.)

Elizabeth Antaya Cardinal Oulette

Born – circa 1783

Married – circa 1807 Jean Marie Cardinal

Married – 17 January 1824 Jean Baptiste Ouimette, at Prairie du Chien[149]

Died – between 17 January 1824 and 21 January 1832[150]

Jean Marie Cardinal and Elizabeth Antaya had five children. The four eldest children were baptized on May 4, 1817, by Father Dunand: Helie, "born January 14, 1810"; Pierre "born December 20, 1812"; and Ustache "born January 20, 1808." Paul baptized on May 5, 1817, but no age or birth date was recorded.[151] Julien, was baptized in 1827 by Father Badin, who recorded his birth as 19 December 1823.[152] (See Jean Baptiste Wemette.)

Françoise Antaya Crelie Courville

Born – circa 1780

Married – Joseph Crelie

Separated from Crelie, circa 1808

Married – before 1817 Pierre Courville[153]

Died – after 1 April 1821[154]

Françoise and Joseph Creilie/Crely had five children: Julie (see below); Marie Louise, born May 12, 1796, and baptized at St. Louis on August 12, 1798; and Therese Josephine, born December 4, 1798, and baptized December 8 at St. Louis. After 1798, Françoise and Joseph moved to Prairie du Chien, where their next two children were baptized.[155]

In April and May 1817, Father Dunand baptized several children of which Françoise was the mother: Joseph Crelis, "fourteen years of age, legal son of Joseph Crelis and Françoise Peltier" (Peltier *dit* Antaya); Josephine Crelie, "eleven years of age, born of the legal marriage of Joseph Crelie and Françoise Antalla" (Antaya).[156]

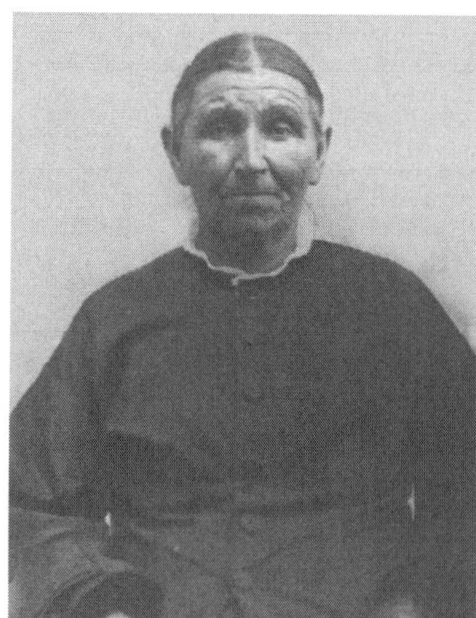

Florence Courville was the daughter of Françoise Antaya Crelie Courville and Pierre Courville. She was born December 1816 and died May 1882 at Duck Creek, Wisconsin. (Private Collection)

Father Dunand also baptized the children born to Françoise and Pierre Courville: Genevieve Courville, "eight years of age, the father being Pierre Courville, the mother being Françoise Crelie, nee Antalla"; Pierre Courville, "six years of age, the father being Pierre

Courville, the mother Françoise Crelis"; Antoine Courville, "about five years of age, the father being Pierre Courville, the mother being Françoise Crelie"; Florence Courville, "born about five months ago, of the legal marriage of Pierre Courville and Françoise Antalla."[157] The last child of Pierre and Françoise Courville was born April 1, 1821, and baptized June 17, 1827. Her name was Françoise, and only her father was present at her baptism.[158] (See Pierre Courville.)

André Bazin

Born – 19 September 1786

Baptized – 26 September 1786 St-Francois-du-Lac, Quebec[159]

Married(?) – Catherine Antaya

Died – 1832/1834[160]

In April 1817, Father Dunand baptized Pierre, "born late July, the father being Andre Bazin, the mother being Catherine Antalla." The godparents were Pierre Lariviere and Marguerite Antalla.[161]

André Bazin of St. François parish in Quebec signed an engagement at Montreal on January 16, 1808, with the Michilimackinac Company to go to Michilimackinac. He then worked for John Blakely on the Mississippi.[162]

Bazin was in Prairie du Chien by the end of the War of 1812. He claimed Village of St. Friole Lot No. 13 and Farm Lot No. 29 in 1820. He had gained the village lot through the Antaya family with his marriage to Catherine. He had purchased the farm lot from John Findley.[163]

Bazin served as a private in Captain Thomas McNair's company of militia formed during the Winnebago War of 1827.[164]

Bazin executed his will on February 29, 1832; the will, written in French, was brought before the Crawford County Probate Court on June 2, 1834. In the will, he left all of his property "both real and personal" to his "friend Pierre Bazin" of Prairie du Chien, who was his son.[165] Pierre died January 10, 1842, and was buried in the St. Gabriel's cemetery the next day.[166]

Louis Gabriel Brisbois

Baptized – 29 April 1817, at Prairie du Chien[167]

Married – 10 January 1827 Judith Provost, at Prairie du Chien[168]

Died – circa 1828

Louis was the son of Michel and Domitille Brisbois. He was born about 1805, as he was twelve years of age when baptized in 1817.[169] He married Judith Provost January 10, 1827, and they had one son, Louis/ Lewis. Louis, the father, died before 1828. On September 21, 1828, Judith Brisbois married François Labatte.[170]

Pierre Courville

Born – 1770s or 1780s in Canada

Married – Françoise Antaya

Married – Marie Antaya Lapointe

Died – after 21 January 1830[171]

Little is known of Pierre. He may be the Pierre Courville who signed an engagement in 1798 to travel from Montreal to Detroit as a devant (the person who guides a canoe) for Henry Berthelet. Henry was a merchant, and the canoe was probably filled with trade goods.[172]

If this is the same Pierre Courville, he was living at Prairie du Chien by 1794, when he occupied Farm Lot No. 10.[173]

Pierre married Françoise Antaya Crelie/Crely. After her death, he married her sister, Marie.[174] (See Françoise Antaya Crely/Crelie Courville.)

Julie Crely Lessard

Born – 2 April 1795

Baptized – 3 December 1796, at St. Louis[175]

Married – 8 May 1817 Pierre Lessort (Lessard), at Prairie du Chien[176]

Died – between 6 August 1827 and 7 April 1831[177]

Julie was the daughter of Joseph Crelie and Françoise Antaya. (See entry for Françoise Antaya Crelie Courville.) Julie was born April 2, 1795, and baptized December 3, 1796, at St. Louis. She married Pierre Lessard, who was born in the Parish of St-Feriol, Province of Quebec. Julie and

Pierre had five children, all of whom were baptized at Prairie du Chien: Pierre, born August 24, 1810; Catherine, born May 11, 1813; Susanne, born February 8, 1815; Ursule, born October 13, 1818; Ignace, born February 22, 1822; and Jean Baptiste, born October 14, 1825. The three eldest children were baptized by Father Dunand in April 1817, and the three youngest were baptized by Father Badin in August 1827.[178]

Therese Chalifoux Gagnier Gauthier

Born – Circa 1809

Baptized – 7 May 1817, eight years of age[179]

Married – 24 November 1823 Regis Gagnier, at Prairie du Chien[180]

Married – circa 1831 Guillaume St. Germain *dit* Gauthier

Died – 1836

Therese was the daughter of Pierre Chalifoux and Lisette, a Sioux woman.[181]

Regis Gagnier and Therese had two children: François and Marie Regis. (See François Regis Gagnier.) After Regis died in 1827, Therese formed a

St. Germain *dit* Gauthier house. The house was owned by Guillaume St. Germain *dit* Gauthier. After Guillaume separated from his wife Magdelaine, he formed a marital relationship with Therese Chalifoux Gagnier, the widow of Regis Gagnier.

relationship with Guillaume St. Germain who had separated from his wife, Magdelaine Brunet St. Germain. Guillaume and Therese had two children: David, born October 14, 1832; and Henriette, born circa 1834. Therese died in 1836 of smallpox.[182]

Marguerite DuBois

Married – 10 February 1817 Joseph Rolette, at Prairie du Chien[183]
Died – before 1818 (See Joseph Rolette.)

Marguerite DuBois was the daughter of Antoine DuBois and a Dakota woman, a relative of Wapasha.[184] Marguerite had been raised by Julien Dubuque. She was fourteen years old when she formed a marital relationship with Joseph Rolette.[185] The couple had three daughters: Emilie, born September 17, 1811; Elizabeth, born November 7, 1813; and Henriette born "December 19, 1813 [sic]." All were baptized by Father Dunand on April 23, 1817.[186]

Marguerite died of consumption.[187]

Claude Gagnier

Born – circa 1798
Baptized – 8 May 1817, at Prairie du Chien[188]
Died – 25 April 1836[189]

Claude Gagnier was the son of Claude Gagnier and Marianne Labuche. When Father Dunand baptized the younger Gagnier in 1817, he recorded that Claude was "nineteen years of age."[190] The younger Gagnier did not marry. Charles Menard, Jr., Gagnier's half-brother, applied to be appointed administrator of his estate. Menard testified that he had provided his brother with "Board, Lodging & Washing" for four years, caring for him in his sickness and burial. Claude Gagnier left a sizeable estate, which included an 80-acre farm and a village lot with house.[191]

Pelagie Gagne/Gagnier

Died – circa 1817

On May 12, 1817, Father Dunand baptized Joseph, the son of François Vertefeuille and Pelagie Gagne.[192]

Pelagie must have died, and François married Marie Chalifous. On August 13, 1827, Father Badin baptized three children born to François Vertefeuille and Marie Chalifous: Catherine, born October 24, 1818; François, born September 22, 1820; and Clemente, born December 12, 1821.[193]

Magdelaine Gauthier

Died – 15 November 1827[194]

On March 2, 1829, Joseph Rolette petitioned the probate court to grant him letters of administration for the estate of Magdelaine Gauthier, who had died November 15, 1827. Rolette stated that he had "furnished her in provisions and clothing and fuel with her family consisting of three person since the month of April 1818 until the month of Nov 1827." He also had paid for the funeral expenses and burial of Magdelaine. Magdelaine's only possession was Farm Lot No. 7.[195]

Joseph Rolette had married Jane Fisher on January 19, 1818. Jane's mother was Magdelaine Gauthier. Magdelaine had married Henry Munro Fisher. They had four children: Henry, Alexander, George, and Jane. Fisher then married Marie Anne Lasaliere at Mackinac on July 22, 1809. Therefore, the supposition has always been that Fisher's first wife, Magdelaine, had died. Fisher had left Prairie du Chien in 1814 with his two eldest sons. He had abandoned his wife, Marie, and their daughter Elizabeth to the care of Marie's family at Michilimackinac. Fisher had left George and Jane in the care of Michel and Domitille Brisbois, their uncle and aunt. George married Genevieve Courville on June 11, 1825.[196] Because Rolette had supported Magdelaine since 1818, this woman may have been Jane Fisher Rolette's mother.

Angelique Giard Lupien

Married – Theodore Lupien

Died – circa 1817

On April 23, 1817, Father Dunand baptized Felicitie Lupien, "five years of age, born of the legal marriage of Theodore Lupien and Angelique Ghair [Giard]."[197] Angelique died sometime before the death of her father, Basile Giard.

Marie Giard Bell

Born – circa 1794

Baptized – 6 May 1817, at Prairie du Chien[198]

Married – 16 May 1825 Tunis Bell, at Prairie du Chien[199]

Died – 1838[200]

Marie was the youngest of three daughters born to Basile Giard. The older girls were Angelique and Marie Louise. When Marie was baptized, Father Dunand recorded her age as twenty-three and stated she was the daughter of Basile Giard and a "Fox woman."[201]

Prudent Langlois

Died – 9 January 1835[202]

Prudent Langlois was from Riviere-du-Loup, Canada. In 1809 and 1810, he signed an engagement to work for one year as a boatman for "Mess. de la Compagnie de Michilimackinac" at Michilimackinac and its dependencies.[203] He was residing at Mackinac when he volunteered in July 1814 to join the force organized to attack the United States fort at Prairie du Chien.[204] At the time of his death, Prudent owed "Madame St. Cire" $6.00 for board and clothing.[205]

Charles Lapointe (Senior)

Born – about 5 February 1788

Married – Suzanne Antaya

Married – Josette Antaya, blessed 8 May 1817, at Prairie du Chien[206]

Married – 3 February 1820 Marie Roc[207]

Died – after 18 November 1831

Charles Lapointe was born at Terrebonne, Canada, the son of François Goddard *dit* Lapointe and Rosalie Miron.[208]

François Lapointe

Born – circa 7 March 1776, Terrebonne, Canada

Married – Marie Antaya, blessed 29 April 1817, at Prairie du Chien[209]

Died – After 1820 census taken and before 9 February 1821[210]

François Lapointe was the son of François Lapointe and Rosalie Miron. He and his two brothers, Charles and Pierre, came to Prairie du Chien about 1785. Lapointe married Marie Antaya, the daughter of Michel Antaya and Marie Menard. Father Dunand sanctified this marriage on April 29, 1817. That same spring Father Dunand baptized five of their children.[211]

By February 20, 1821, Lapointe had died, for on that date an inventory of his estate was presented to Wilfred Owen, Justice of the Peace.[212] His estate was sizeable and included a lot in the Village of St. Friole on which was the family home, a horse mill, and a barn. Lapointe also owned Farm Lot No. 37. It took several years to settle the estate. When closed, his widow, Marie, received the front portion of Farm Lot No. 37 "during her life for Dower," with the remainder going to "the four youngest children to wit: Bartholimi, Hyacinthe, St. Luke, and Rosalie." The village lot, with buildings, was "assigned to François, Michael, Magdelaine & Joachim, the eldest children."[213]

Joachim Lapointe

Born – circa 1813 or 5 January 1810[214]

Baptized – 25 April 1817, at Prairie du Chien[215]

Married – 8 January 1836 Ursule Lavigne *dit* Gauthier[216]

Died – 1836[217]

Joachim Lapointe was the son of François Lapointe and Marie Antaya. He was baptized by Father Dunand, who recorded that Joachim was "four years of age."[218] When his father's estate was undergoing probate in 1830, Joachim's mother, Marie Antaya, testified that Joachim was born "on the fifth day of January one thousand eight hundred and ten." Hyacinth St. Cire corroborated Marie's testimony.[2198]

Joachim Lapointe died in April 1836, intestate and without heirs. His brother, Bartholomew, petitioned the Court to be appointed administrator. Ursule, his wife, also petitioned the Court. She asked the judge to "allow her anything out of the property of the said deceased." Joachim owned no land, though his estate included a "lot of house logs." The livestock and farm tools he owned were sold at auction and his clothing sold at a separate auction.[220]

Pierre Lapointe

Born – 1747-1750[221]

Married – circa 1784 Etonkasahwee[222]

Died – circa 1821[223]

According to his testimony in 1820, Lapointe was "seventy years old; that he has been forty-four years in the country, of which period he has resided thirty-eight years at Prairie du Chien; that in the year seventeen hundred and eighty-one, this deponent was at Michilimackinac, and acted in the capacity of interpreter at the treaty held by Governor Sinclair with the Indians, for the purchase of the island of Michilimackinac, Green Bay, and Prairie du Chien." Lapointe's testimony in 1820 helped those who claimed ownership of farm lots on the south end of the prairie and lots within the Main Village gain title to their lands.[224]

Pierre and Etonkasahwee had two daughters: Pelagie and Therese. About 1803, Pelagie entered into a marital relationship with Lewis Crawford, a British trader. After his death, she married Antoine Lachapelle.[225]

Pierre Lapointe died about 1821.[226]

Suzanne Lapointe Lessard Morrel

Born – 20 March 1816, at Prairie du Chien

Baptized – 24 April 1817, at Prairie du Chien[227]

Married – 7 April 1831 Pierre Lessard, at Prairie du Chien[228]

Married – 1 September 1835 Joseph Morrel, at Prairie du Chien[229]

Died – between September 1837 and May 1838[230]

Suzanne was the daughter of Charles Lapointe and Josette Antaya. Pierre and Suzanne had one child, Julie.[231]

Michel Lariviere

Born – circa 1806

Baptized – 2 May 1817 at age eleven, at Prairie du Chien[232]

Married – 10 September 1827 Catherine Roc, at Prairie du Chien[233]

Married – Catherine Roc, marriage blessed 13 May 1829, at Prairie du Chien[234]
Died – October 1834[235]

Michel Lariviere was "born of the legal marriage of Pierre Lariviere and Marguerite Antalla [Antaya]."[236] Lariviere and his family lived on and farmed part of Farm Lot No. 30, which had been claimed by and granted to his father. Lariviere left behind his widow and two children, Pierre and Isadore. Catherine received "sundry articles as set off" by court decree and one third of Michel's personal property after his debts had been paid. François Lapointe was appointed guardian of Pierre and Isadore.[237]

Joseph Lessard

Died – 1835[238]

On September 8, 1835, Pierre Lariviere presented an inventory of the estate of Joseph Lessard to the Court. The estate amounted to only a pair of wheels and a horse cart painted green with one wheel "much damaged by use." The shaft for the cart was broken and the wheels had no iron. The total value was $21.00. The next day Joseph Morrel was appointed guardian of Julie Lessard, a minor.[239] (See Suzanne Lapointe Lessard Morrell.)

Pierre Lessard

Baptized – 6 February 1787 at Ste-Anne-de-Beaupre[240]
Married – 8 May 1817 Julie Crely, at Prairie du Chien[241]
Married – 7 April 1831 Susanne Lapointe, at Prairie du Chien[242]
Died – 28 February 1834[243]

Pierre Lessard died without a will. His wife, Suzanne, was appointed administratrix of the estate. She first petitioned the court "to Grant her what property that you will draw and find just." Lessard's estate was extensive. He farmed and traded with the American Fur Company. His house was well-furnished, and gauging by the tools, wood, shingles, and paint supplies that were part of his estate, Lessard may have built houses for residents of the prairie and also been a carpenter with cabinetmaking skills. But he also was in debt to others. Suzanne Lessard had to petition the court again. She stated she had "no means to pay for her support this winter." Therefore, she asked the court to extend the settlement of the estate until the first day of May next [1835]."[244] (See Hardin Perkins, for whom Lessard made a coffin.)

Louis Barrette presented a bill to Lessard's estate for $20.00 "for making railing around grave."[245]

(See Julie Crely Lessard and Suzanne Lapointe Lessard Morrel.)

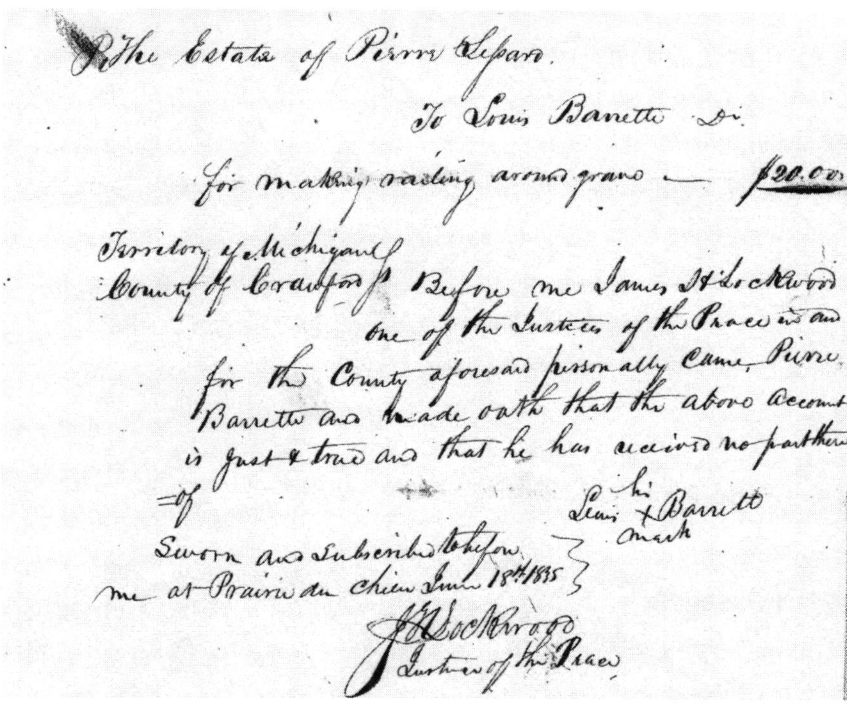

The Estate of Pierre Lessard

To Louis Barrette Dr.

for making railing around grave — $20.00

Territory of Michigan
County of Crawford Before me James H. Lockwood one of the Justices of the Peace in and for the County aforesaid personally Came, Pierre Barrette and made oath that the above account is just & true and that he has received no part thereof

Louis his x mark Barrette

Sworn and Subscribed before me at Prairie du Chien June 18th 1835

J. H. Lockwood
Justice of the Peace

Bill from Louis Barrette for making the wood railing that would have been placed around the grave of Pierre Lessard. June 18, 1835.

Theodore W. Lupien *dit* Bore

Born – 17 March 1781, Louiseville, Maskinonge, Quebec

Baptized – 18 March 1781[246]

Married – circa 1811 Angelique Giard

Married – 16 May 1817 Therese Crelie, at Prairie du Chien[247]

Died – 1818, Prairie du Chien

When Father Dunand married Théodore and Therese, he recorded that Théodore Lupien was the son of Antoine Lupin and Madeline Brule, native of Canada.[248] In 1804, Lupien signed an engagement to work in "dependences des pay d'en haut" (the dependencies of the back county) for James & Andrew McGill & Company, fur traders headquartered in Montreal.[249] Lupien first married Angelique, a daughter of Basile Giard and then married Therese, the daughter of Joseph Crelie and Françoise Peltier *dit* Antalla. Théodore and Therese had one child, also named Théodore. After Lupien's death, Therese married Pierre Paquette.[250]

Xavier and Jean Baptiste Paquette

Born – before 1828

According to Moses Paquette, the son of Pierre Paquette and Therese Josephine Crelie, he had two older brothers: Xavier and Jean Baptiste. Pierre married Therese in 1818, after the death of her husband Théodore W. Lupien. The two Paquette boys were infants "who died within a day or two of each other, before my birth. (Moses was born March 4, 1828, in Portage.) Xavier and Jean Baptiste were buried in the Catholic cemetery at Prairie du Chien."[251]

Hardin Perkins

Married – 31 May 1823 Elizabeth Courtois, at Prairie du Chien[252]

Died - 15 February 1826[253]

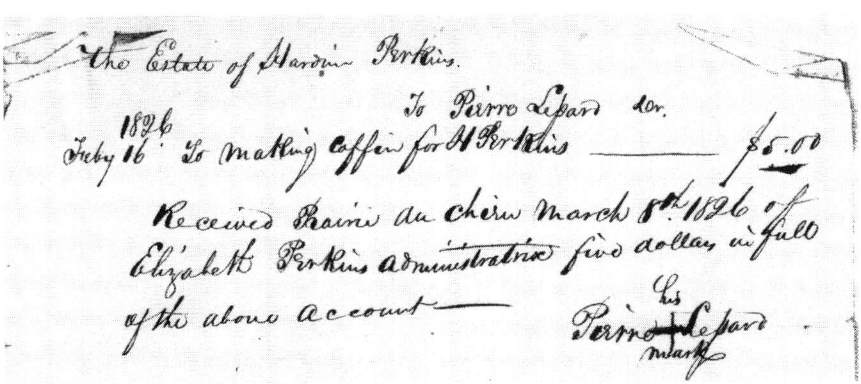

The Estate of Hardin Perkins.

To Pierre Lessard Dr.

1826
Feby 16 To making coffin for H Perkins —— $5.00

Received Prairie du chien march 8th 1826 of Elizabeth Perkins administratrix five dollars in full of the above account ——

his
Pierre + Lessard
mark

Bill from Pierre Lessard for making a coffin for Hardin Perkins. February 16, 1826.

Hardin and Elizabeth had two children: Charles, born April 24, 1824; and Marie, born March 25, 1826. Both were baptized in 1827 by Father Badin.[254]

Hardin died, having made a will and appointing his wife, Elizabeth, administratrix of his estate. Elizabeth paid Pierre Lessard $5.00 for making a coffin, and two men $1.00 for digging the grave.[255]

Alexis Pizanne

Born – 15 March 1827, at Prairie du Chien[256]

Baptized – 29 May 1827, at Prairie du Chien[257]

Died – prior to 6 December 1836

Alexis was the second child of Edward and Margaret Campbell Pizanne. On December 6, 1839, Margaret sold "all her right, title, interest, claim or demand in the land known as the Half-Breed Tract on the west shore of the Mississippi River to her children, Charles, Emily, and George."[258] Alexis was not listed as one of Margaret's children; he likely had died by the time Margaret had sold her rights.

Strange Powers (Poze)

Born – 10 June 1786, Sorel, Canada

Baptized – 3 August 1786[259]

Married – 14 May 1825 Euphrosine Antaya, at Prairie du Chien[260]

Died – 27 November 1837, Prairie du Chien

Strange Powers was born June 10, 1786, and baptized at Christ Church Anglican, Sorel, Canada on August 3, 1786; he was the son of John and Magdalene Powers. He had settled at Prairie du Chien by 1816 and worked as a baker in the household of Michel Brisbois. In 1818, Strange Powers and Euphrosine Antaya Fraser formed a marital relationship. Euphrosine had not been divorced from her husband James Fraser, who had left her and moved to Drummond Island. James Duane Doty, justice for the Michigan Territorial Circuit Court in Crawford County, indicted Powers for fornication in 1824. Euphrosine petitioned the court for a divorce from Fraser, which was granted in 1825. Strange Powers

Euphrosine Antaya Fraser Powers (1796-1867). Euphrosine was the daughter of Pierre and Catherine Antaya. She married Strange Powers. In 1836, Strange and Euphrosine donated land for the construction of a church. The church structure was named St. Gabriel's. (The Powers-Barrette Family)

and Euphrosine Antaya were then married by James H. Lockwood, Justice of the Peace.[261]

Powers purchased Lot No. 14 in the Village of St. Friole from his brother-in-law, Pierre Lariviere, who lived on Lot. No. 15. Houses, dating to the late 1700s-early 1800s stood on both lots. Powers also purchased several farm lots. When McNair's Company of Michigan Militia formed in July 1827, Powers served as sergeant of the company.[262]

On February 2, 1836, Powers sold a tract of land, which was part of Farm Lot No. 28, to Bishop Frederic Rese of the Diocese of Detroit.[263] St. Gabriel's Church was built upon the land and a cemetery placed behind the church structure. When Powers died, he owned Farm Lots Nos. 28, 34, and 35 and Lot No. 14 in the Village of St. Friole.[264]

Strange Powers House. Within the structure is the original log home of Strange and Euphrosine Powers.

Strange and Euphrosine Powers had seven children: Harriet, born September 18, 1819, and baptized as Helene; Euphrosine, born February 13, 1821; Jean Baptiste (John), born October 10, 1826; George, born May 15, 1828; Caroline, born April 1830; Jane, born circa 1830; and Adrian, born July 1831. The three eldest were baptized by Father Badin.[265]

According to Samuel Barrette, a grandson of Strange and Euphrosine Powers, Powers was buried "north of the Gardepie lot" in the Old Catholic Burying Ground. A pile of stones once marked his burial place.[266]

Etienne Précour

Died — before 20 November 1820.

On that date, an inventory was taken of the estate of Etienne Précour.[267]

Précour was born at Beloeil, Quebec April 23, 1775, the son of François Degré *dit* Précour and Marie Anne Jarret *dit* Beauregard.[268] In 1807, Précour was at Michilimackinac and on July 21 signed an engagement to work for Rocheblave and Pollier on the Missouri River.[269] Précour married Catherine, the widow of Pierre Antaya, who had died in 1805. Their marriage was blessed at Prairie du Chien by Father Dunand on May 12, 1817.[270]

François Provost

Married – 29 April 1817 Theotiste Antalla (Antaya), at Prairie du Chien[271]

Died – 19 April 1840[272]

François Provost was the son of François Prevost and Madeline Laporte of Canada.[273] On April 29, 1817, Father Dunand married François Provost and Theotiste Antalla (Antaya). Theotiste was baptized the same day she was married, her age given as twenty-two; she was the daughter of Pierre Antalla and Catherine, a Sioux woman.[274] The marriage solemnized a union that had existed for several years. Three days later, Father Dunand baptized the couple's seven-year-old daughter, Judith.[275] Not until ten years later would their other children be baptized. In 1827, Father Badin baptized Marguerite, born January 25, 1818, and Magdelaine, born February 24, 1820.[276]

Marguerite Provost

Born – 25 January 1818[277]
Baptized – 13 August 1827, at Prairie du Chien[278]
Married – 5 August 1835 Hyacinthe Lapointe, at Prairie du Chien[279]
Died – before 16 April 1839 when Hyacinthe married Susan Molson[280]

Marguerite Provost was the daughter of François Provost and Theotiste Peltier *dit* Entailla (Antaya).[281]

Jean Marie Queré

Died – 1 December 1825[282]

Queré provided testimony for many people who were claiming ownership of their lands at Prairie du Chien in 1820. In several of the claims, Queré stated that he had "been thirty-three years in this country." Queré gained title to Farm Lot No. 32, which he occupied from "1797 to the present [1820]" and Upper Village Lot No. 16.[283]

On November 22, 1802, Jean Marie Queré was appointed an ensign in the St. Clair County regimental militia of the Indiana territory. Prairie du Chien was part of St. Clair County.[284]

Louise Queré, identified as "Consort of Jean M. Queré" informed the probate court that Queré had "left a will leaving to your petitioner heir to all his property."[285]

Armoire owned by Jean Marie Queré. This piece of furniture had been part of the furnishings of Queré home. Upon Jean Marie's death, the armoire passed to his wife Louise. (Private Collection)

Edmond Ranger

Married – 28 February 1824 Louise Lapointe, at Prairie du Chien[286]

Died – between December 1824 and August 1827[287]

Veronique, the daughter of Edmond Ranger and Louise Lapointe was born December 12, 1824. On August 13, 1827, Joseph Deschamp and Louise Lapointe were united in marriage at Prairie du Chien. Father Badin recorded that Louise was the "widow of Emond [sic] Ranger... Joseph recognizes as his adoptive daughter Veronique Ranger, daughter of his wife."[288]

John Simpson

Married – 12 May 1817 Josephine (Josette) Peltier, at Prairie du Chien[289]

Died – before September 1835

John Simpson was the son of John Simpson and Marie McIntosh, a native of Canada. Of Scots heritage, Simpson may have been one of the people to whom Father Dunand gave instructions in the Catholic faith and then married him and Josephine Peltier in the Catholic Church on May 12, 1817.[290]

Josette Simpson married Alexis Crochiere on September 28, 1835.[291] It may be assumed that John Simpson died before that date and as a Catholic was buried in the Old Catholic Cemetery. This is further supported by the fact that Father Lucien Galtier buried Josette in "the old C. grave yard, upon her expressed request before dying."[292] (See Josette Crochiere.)

François Vertefeuille

Born – Louiseville, Maskinongé, Quebec

Baptized – 21 March 1774[293]

Married – Pelagie Gagné/Gagnier[294]

Married – 7 May 1824 Marie Chalifous, at Prairie du Chien[295]

Died – prior to 1840

François Vertefeuille was the son of Joseph Vanasse Vertefeuille and Rose Pelland.[296] By 1790, Vertefeuille chose to work in the fur trade. In 1797, he signed an engagement to work for Parker, Gerrard & Ogilvy as a voyageur. In 1803, he worked for two seasons at Grand Portage for Alexander Mackenzie. In 1807 and 1808, he would paddle a canoe from Montreal to Michilimackinac to Fort Kaministiguiâ on the north shore of Lake Superior. He worked for McTavish, Frobisher & Company and John Ogilvy and Roderick Mackenzie. In 1809 and 1811, he worked for the Michilimackinac Company. On these engagements, François' last name was recorded as Vertefeuille or Vanasse *dit* Vertefeuille.[297]

By 1809, Vertefeuille had decided to make a home at Prairie du Chien. In that year, he enclosed and improved Farm Lot No. 21. Within a short time, he also acquired Upper Village Lot No. 4, on which a house had already been constructed. He then constructed a barn on his farm lot. When the residents of Prairie du Chien needed to establish a new location for the community burying ground in 1816, Vertefeuille donated part of this farm lot. In 1826, he sold his house to his daughter, Marie Louise Vertefeuille Dyonne. Vertefeuille is included in the 1830 Federal census of Prairie du Chien, and Etienne and Marie Louise Dyonne are included in the territorial census of 1834. But after that date none of the members of the Vertefeuille and Dyonne families reside at Prairie du Chien.[298]

François Vertefeuille House located on Upper Village Lot No. 4. François donated part of his farm lot for the Old Catholic Burying Ground.

On May 12, 1817, Father Dunand baptized Joseph, the son of François Vertefeuille and Pelagie Gagné. Children of François Vertefeuille and Marie Chalifous included: Marie Louise, married in 1823 to Etienne Dyonne; François, born September 22, 1820; Catherine, born 24, 1818; and Clemente, born December 12, 1821. The three were baptized on August 13, 1827, by Father Badin.[299]

Jean Baptiste Wemette, Jr.

Married – 17 January 1824 Elizabeth Antaille, at Prairie du Chien[300]
Died – about 17 July 1829[301]

Jean Baptiste Wemette, Jr. was the son of Jean Baptiste Wemet/Wemette/Ouillette. Jean Baptiste Ouillette married Elizabeth Antaille, the widow of Jean Marie Cardinal on January 17, 1824.[302]

On July 18, 1829, Joseph Brisbois presented a petition to the Crawford County Judge of Probate. In the petition he stated "that Baptiste Wemette [the son] Administrator on the estate of Baptiste Wemette Sr. Just departed this life...." Therefore, Brisbois asked to be appointed administrator of both estates. Dr. William Beaumont had visited

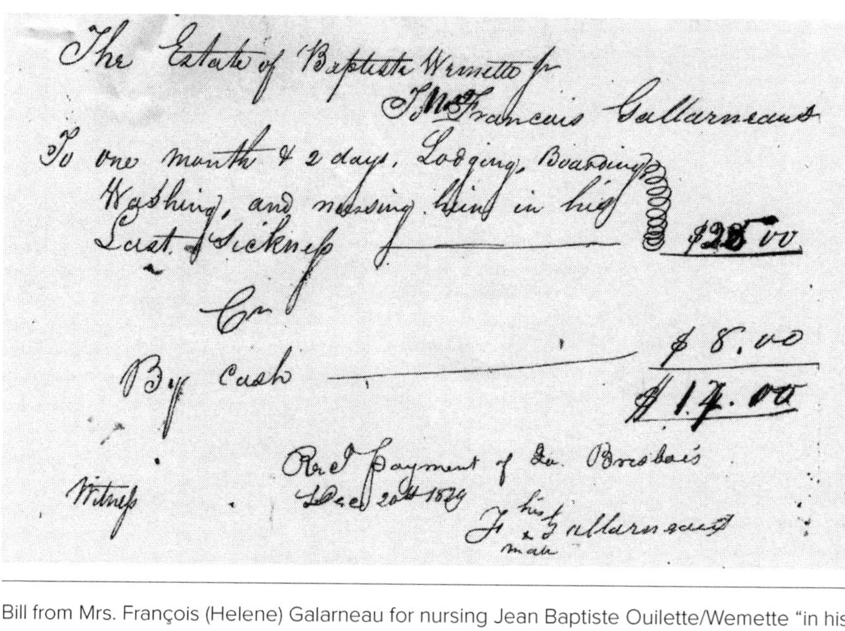

The Estate of Baptiste Wemette Jr
To Mrs Francois Gallarneau
To one month & 2 days, Lodging, Boarding, Washing, and nursing him in his Last Sickness — $25 00
Cr
By cash — $8.00
$17.00
Recd payment of Jo. Brisbois
Decr 20th 1829
Witness
his
F x Gallarneau
mark

Bill from Mrs. François (Helene) Galarneau for nursing Jean Baptiste Ouilette/Wemette "in his last sickness." December 20, 1829.

Wemette, Jr. from October 1828 until July 17, 1829; and during the months of January, February, and March, Beaumont had maintained Wemette, Jr. in the Fort Crawford post hospital. Wemette, Jr. may have been too ill to live in his house. François St. Jean cared for Wemette, Jr. for one month and then François Galarneau and his wife, Helene, cared for Wemette, Jr. for one month and two days "in his Last Sickness."[303]

Jean Baptiste Pion made the coffin for the burial of Wemette, the son, and furnished the planks at a cost of $7.00.[304] (See Jean Baptiste Wemet [Senior].)

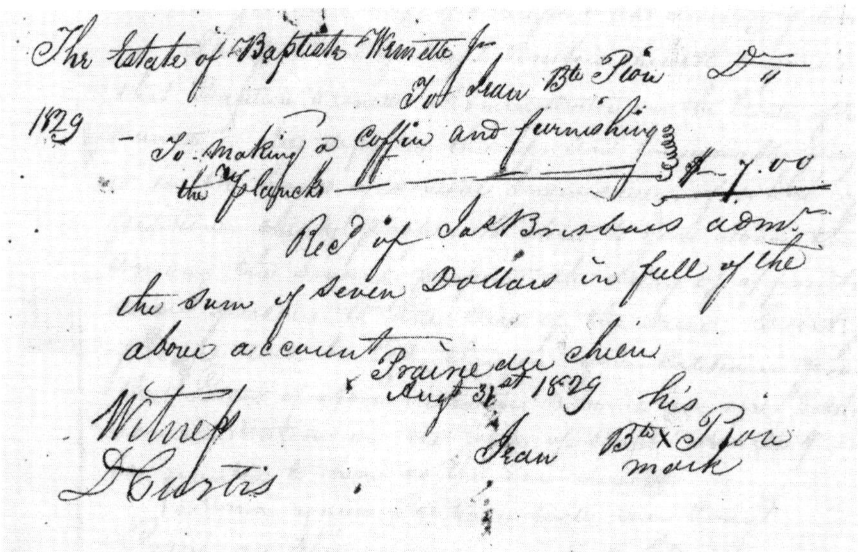
The Estate of Baptiste Wemette Jr
To Jean Bte Pion Dr
1829 — To making a Coffin and furnishing the planks — $7.00
Recd of Jos Brisbois admr. the sum of Seven Dollars in full of the above account
Prairie du Chien Aug 31st 1829
Witness J. Curtis
his Jean Bte X Pion mark

Bill from Jean Baptiste Pion for "making a coffin and furnishing the planks" for the burial of Jean Baptiste Wemette, Jr.

People Not Buried in the Old Catholic Burying Ground, Though Names are Listed on the 1967 Plaque

Charles Bazin

No person named Charles Bazin is on record having lived in Crawford County. This may have been a mistake, and the name possibly was meant to be André Bazin, who died circa 1832-1834. (See André Bazin.)

Charles Brisbois

Born – 8 March 1798[305]

Married – circa 1832 Ann C. Smith

Died – 13 August 1847

Charles was the son of Michel and Domitille Brisbois. While employed by the Hudson's Bay Company, he met and married Ann Smith, who had been born at Hudson Bay in Canada.[306] By 1844, Charles and his family had returned to Prairie du Chien. The declaration of war against Mexico necessitated the withdrawal of U.S. troops from Fort Crawford. Congress told Wisconsin territorial governor Henry Dodge to raise volunteers to man the post. A company of volunteers, known as "Dodge Guards," was enrolled on June 25, 1826. Wiram Knowlton was appointed captain and Charles Brisbois lieutenant. While serving, Charles became ill and died. A memorial ribbon was produced which stated:

IN MEMORY OF LIEUT. CHARLES BRISBOIS,
WHO DEPARTED THIS LIFE, AUG. 13, 1847.

"Of congestive ills, at Fort. Crawford, on Friday evening, the 13th inst., Charles Brisbois, first lieutenant of the volunteers, stationed at this post, aged forty-nine years, five months and thirteen days. The disease of which Mr. Brisbois died, was contracted when on a visit to St. Louis, and in the fatal termination, the community has lost one of the most valuable citizens, and society an honored member. He was born and educated in the western country, and from youth to manhood had been engaged in the fur trade, connected with the Hudson Bay Fur Company. Residing in a country where there was no law, he had ever acted upon principles of right, and formed a character, which in later years, in his intercourse with men, had won for him the confidence and respect of all. In July, last year, he became second lieutenant of the Dodge Guards, and has since been promoted to first lieutenant, which office he filled at the time of his death. As a soldier, his upright and impartial conduct had secured the confidence of his superiors in rank, and the respect of all under his command; as a citizen, he was liberal and active; as a friend, faithful, generous and kind. He has left a wife and family, and a large number of relatives and friends to mourn their loss. His funeral took place on Saturday evening, with military honors, and a large concourse of people were in attendance, and joined in the solemn ceremony that consigned to their last resting place, the earthly remains of an esteemed friend, a kind husband and father and a worthy citizen."

His grave, and that of his wife, are marked by headstones in St. Gabriel's Cemetery.

_____ Caya 1819

Michel Caya was born March 21, 1823, in Quebec, the son of François Caya and Marie Luce Chassé. He was baptized March 23, 1823, at Baie-du-Fabvre, Quebec.[307] According to a biographical sketch, Mitchell (as he came to be known) "was the first permanent settler in the town of Seneca. He came first in the spring of 1846, but did not make his [land] entry till two years later.... He came at the solicitation of his brother, who had preceded him to Prairie du Chien two years earlier." Michel married Rose Mary Loyer on November 7, 1842. All members of the Caya family in Crawford County have descended from Michel. Michel died May 12, 1893, and is buried in Seattle, Washington.[308] So, it has not been possible to determine the listing of "Caya 1819."

François Chenevert

Born – 10 April 1785 at Yamaska, Quebec

Married – Marie Louise Giard at Prairie du Chien[309]

Buried – 1858 St. Gabriel's Cemetery[310]

Dan Gallarneau

Unable to be identified.

Meringer Hermeranger

After the death of Charles Brisbois (see Charles Brisbois), Ann, his widow, married Charles Hermeranger. Hermeranger was a blacksmith and had been born in Wisconsin circa 1825. The name has been spelled many ways including Maranger and Ermeranger. Hermeranger died December 12, 1888, age sixty-five years. Ann died November 4, 1878, age fifty-nine years. Both are buried in St. Gabriel's Cemetery, with stones marking their graves.[311]

Joe Kapl

Unable to be identified.

Jean Baptiste L'Emerie

Baptized – 9 December 1768 at Verchères, Quebec[312]

Married –28 December 1818 Adelaide Gagnier at Prairie du Chien

Marriage Blessed – 16 August 1827 at Prairie du Chien[313]

Buried – 22 February 1846 St Gabriel's Cemetery[314]

Joe Legree

Unable to be identified.

Claude Menard

Unable to be identified.

John (Jean Baptiste) Prince

Jean Baptiste and Baptiste Prince are listed in the 1850 federal census as residing in Prairie du Chien. Jean Baptiste was born 1829-1831 in Red River, Manitoba, Canada. Baptiste was born in Canada. Both stated their occupation as laborer.[315]

Baptiste was buried July 21, 1853 "age 81 years." Jean Baptiste was buried February 11, 1855 "age 26 years." Both men are buried in St. Gabriel's Cemetery.[316]

Jacques Reed

This may be James Reed. If so, James Reed died June 3, 1875, at Trempealeau, Wisconsin. His age was recorded as "79 years and 5 months."[317]

James Reed was born in Kentucky. He enlisted in the U.S. Army in 1814 and was assigned to the Rifle Regiment. In June 1817, he was assigned to Fort Crawford at Prairie du Chien and served until November 1819. He then applied for and was given the position as post sutler (a civilian authorized to maintain a store on the post and sell provisions to soldiers stationed there).[318]

Reed married Margaret of the Chippeway on May 12, 1823. He then married Agather Wood on July 14, 1831. He married Archange Grignon on October 5, 1844. On the marriage records, he was listed as Jacques.[319]

In 1830, James Reed was issued a license to trade at "The Mountain in the Water" (Trempealeau). According to Antoine Grignon, his stepson, James built a house at Trempealeau.[320]

Thomas Rivard

Unable to be identified.

Charles Rivaux

Unable to be identified.

Laurent Rolette

Born – circa 1799

Buried – 11 October 1849, St. Gabriel's Cemetery[321]

Laurent was the younger brother of Joseph Rolette. In the 1820s, he lived and traded at Michilimackinac with Joseph supplying him trade goods.[322] Laurent Rolette later traded at English Prairie on the Wisconsin River (near Muscoda) and clerked for Pierre Paquette.

Hyacinthe St. Cyr

Born – 27 June 1784 at St. Louis

Married – 1819 Marie-Anne at St. Louis[323]

Married – 8 May 1824 Melanie Gagnier at Prairie du Chien[324]

Buried – 22 January 1849, St. Gabriel's Cemetery[325]

Pierre Paquette

Born – 1798, St. Louis, Missouri

Married – 1818 Therese Josephine Crely Lupien, at St. Louis

Died – 18 October 1836, at the Fox-Wisconsin Portage[326]

Pierre Paquette was born in St. Louis. He made a home at Prairie du Chien for a short time with his wife, Therese Crely, and then around 1818, he moved to the portage of the Fox and Wisconsin Rivers, later named Portage, Wisconsin. For several years, he worked as an agent for Joseph Rolette and the American Fur Company. He conducted a trading post and a transportation service between the two rivers.

Paquette was known for his physical strength and fluency in French, English, and several Indian languages. He frequently acted as a Ho-Chunk interpreter at the treaty meetings of the 1820s and 1830s. During the Black Hawk War, he served as a government scout and participated in the Battle of Wisconsin Heights near Sauk City. He later served as translator for Henry Dodge.[327]

After the conclusion of a council between Governor Dodge (representing the United States) and the Ho-Chunk, an altercation occurred between Paquette and Mah-zah-mah-nee-kah, known as Iron Walker. Both men were intoxicated. Paquette went to the home of Iron Walker. Iron Walker told Paquette to come no further. If he advanced another step, he would shoot Paquette. Paquette dared Iron Walker to shoot him, and Iron Walker shot Paquette, who died immediately. Satterlee Clark, who was present at the altercation, buried Paquette at the portage.[328]

At the time of Paquette's death, the portage was part of Crawford County. The county seat was Prairie du Chien, so Paquette's estate was probated in Prairie du Chien. Though Paquette's estate was probated at Prairie du Chien, Paquette died and was buried at the portage.

Edward Pizanne

Born and baptized – 10 October 1784, Sorel, Canada[329]
Married – before 1823 Victoire Lapointe
Married – 7 June 1824 Margaret (Pelagie) Campbell, at Prairie du Chien[330]
Marriage blessed – 31 July 1827[331]
Died – 1836, at Fort Winnebago

Edward Pizanne was the son of Nicolas Michel Pizanne and Victoire Benoit of Sorel, Quebec. On July 20, 1808, Pizanne signed an engagement to work for the Michilimackinac Company to go to la Baye (Green Bay). He was rehired the following year and then on August 5, 1811, Jacques Porlier hired Pizanne to go to the Mississippi.[332]

At Prairie du Chien, Edward Pizanne married Victoire Lapointe, according to Therese Lapointe Barrette. The burial of Victoire Bizanne was recorded in 1823 (see above). Edward Pizanne and Margaret Campbell were married by a magistrate on June 7, 1824. Edward and Margaret had two sons, Charles and Alexis. On May 29, 1827, the two boys were baptized, and a month later, on June 30, Marguerite was baptized. Her age was given as 22, and she was registered as the daughter of John Campbell, a U.S. Indian agent who had died in 1807, and Ninse, a Sioux (Dakota) woman. After her baptism, Father Badin sanctified their marriage on July 31, 1827.[333]

Edward Pizanne became employed by the American Fur Company and worked for the Upper Mississippi Outfit. The winter of 1823-1824, Pizanne received goods from Joseph Rolette to trade above the Falls of St. Anthony among the Folle Avoine (Ojibwe).[334]

After that winter, Pizanne established a trading site at Trempealeau. Lewis Cass, Governor of Michigan Territory, issued a license for Pizanne to trade at Montagne qui tremps a L'eau in 1826. Joseph Street, U.S. Indian agent at Prairie du Chien, issued a license to Pizanne in 1830. Lawrence Taliaferro, U.S. Indian Agent at Fort Snelling, issued a license for Pizanne to trade at "The Mountain in the Water" in 1832.[335]

In the summer of 1836, Pizanne and two or three men traveled to the portage (between the Fox and Wisconsin Rivers). Pizanne fell ill and died at the portage sometime before October 24, 1836, when Hercules L. Dousman petitioned the Probate Court in Crawford County to be appointed administrator of the estate of Edward Pizanne.[336]

Though his estate was probated at Prairie du Chien, Edward Pizanne died and was buried at the portage.

Deaths between 1817 and 1840 of Men with no Association with the Catholic Faith

Father Marie Joseph Dunand recorded that on May 10, 1817, he performed a "blessing of the parish cemetery." While there was no formally organized parish at Prairie du Chien, Father Dunand probably considered the baptized Catholic residents of the prairie a parish.[337]

There is nothing in canon law in the 1800s, or now, that prevented a person not baptized into the Catholic faith from being buried in a Catholic cemetery. Until 1842, when the Lowertown Cemetery was opened, the Old Catholic Burying Ground and St. Gabriel's Cemetery were the only formalized burying grounds at Prairie du Chien. So, men and women not of the Catholic faith who died at Prairie du Chien before 1840 or 1842 may have been buried in the old burying ground.

James Aird

Born – ?

Married –

Died – 27 February 1819, at Prairie du Chien

Little is known of the early life of James Aird. He was born in Scotland, and like many young Scotsmen, he left his country to find work in the North American fur trade. He was in Quebec in 1778 and then the trading region of Michilimackinac. By 1786, his principal location was Prairie du Chien. He traded with the Dakota on the St. Peters (Minnesota) River and westward into Spanish territory along the tributaries of the upper Missouri River. In 1805, Aird became part of Robert Dickson and Company, continuing to trade along the Missouri River.

As late as 1810, Aird was still hiring men at Michilimackinac for service on the Missouri, but about that time he himself returned to the upper Mississippi. In 1807, Robert Dickson and Company had become a part of the recently organized Michilimackinac Company and, in the winter of 1810–11, Aird was trading for this company above the Falls of St. Anthony with his brother, George Aird, and Robert Dickson.[338]

James Aird and *Mar-pi-ya-ro-to-win* (Grey Cloud), a daughter of the Dakota chief Wahpasha, had one daughter, Margaret.[339]

After the end of the War of 1812, Aird traded for the American Fur Company.[340]

At the time of his death, Aird owned: a farm on which there was a house, a stable, two barns and a horse mill; a farm of 100 acres with a house and two barns; a farm of 200 acres with a house; and a lot in the Main Village with two dwelling houses, a bake house, and stable.[341]

Henry Munro Fisher

Born – 14 November 1776[342]
Married – circa 1796 Magdelaine Gauthier
Married – 22 July 1809 Marie Anne LaSaliere[343]
Died – 1827 or 1838 (?)

Henry Munro Fisher was the son of Donald and Elizabeth Munro Fisher and was born in Hebron, New York.[344] He was raised in Montreal, and at the age of sixteen, his mother apprenticed him to Isaac Todd. A fur trader, Todd sent Fisher to Michilimackinac as his representative. Fisher followed the trade to Prairie du Chien and within a short time made his home on Main Village Lot No. 6. He was commissioned a captain in the St. Clair County militia in 1802. When Lt. Zebulon M. Pike explored the upper Mississippi River in 1804-1805, Pike boarded with Fisher while he stayed at Prairie du Chien. When Illinois Territory was formed in 1809, Fisher was appointed a justice of the peace.

In the summer of 1814, an American force under the command of Governor William Clark took possession of Prairie du Chien and built a fort in the Main Village. Henry Munro Fisher had supported the British and traded in Montreal. Fisher left Prairie du Chien for the Red River with his two oldest sons, Henry and Alexander, and Charles, a son of Michel Brisbois. Fisher left his youngest son, George, and his only daughter, Genevieve (she came to be known as Jane), in the care of Michel and Domitille Brisbois. Domitille Brisbois and Madeline Fisher were sisters. Fisher became the quartermaster of the British Indian Department.[345]

He returned to Prairie du Chien in 1823 and died at the home of his daughter, Jane Fisher Rolette in 1827.[346] Henry Munro Fisher's estate was not probated until 1838.[347]

Solomon Leipcap

Born – circa 1773, Pennsylvania[348]

Died – 28 June 1827, at Prairie du Chien

At the age of thirty-five, Solomon Leipcap enlisted in the U.S. Army in Lancaster, Pennsylvania for a term of five years. He stated that he was from Newtown, Berks County and his occupation was "Farmer." Leipcap was posted to Detroit and then to Prairie du Chien. He spent most of his enlistment at Fort Snelling.[349] When his enlistment was finished, he stayed in the Northwest and by 1827 lived at Prairie du Chien.

On June 28, 1827, Leipcap was working for Registre Gagnier. Gagnier farmed part of the land owned by his half-brother François Ducquouette, which was located at the south end of Prairie du Chien. On that day, Gagnier and Leipcap were killed by Red Bird and his companions.[350]

Father Badin recorded that he buried Registre Gagnier in the parish cemetery (Old Catholic Burying Grounds) on June 29, 1827. He did not note whether Solomon Leipcap was also buried in the cemetery.[351]

Burials in the Brisbois Cemetery

Michel Brisbois

Born – 17 October 1760, Yamaska, Quebec[352]

Married – Cham-brey-win-kaw[353]

Married – 6 August 1796, Domitille Gauthier, at Michilimackinac[354]

Died – 1 April 1837, at Prairie du Chien[355]

Michel Brisbois was the son of Joseph Dubois *dit* Brisebois and Marguerite Nault.[356] He attended school in Montreal, then like many young men sought employment in the fur trade. An educated man, he was not a voyageur or engagé, but operated as an independent fur trader. By 1778 he was working out of Michilimackinac. He had a marital relationship with Cham-brey-win-kaw, and they had three children: Michel, Angelique, and Antoine. Brisbois then settled at Prairie du Chien. He obviously was a well-respected man in this community. In 1781, the residents of the prairie realized they needed title to the land at the prairie. They met and selected three men to travel to Mackinac and request from the British Governor title to their property. Michel Brisbois witnessed the signing of the document prepared by Lt. Governor Patrick Sinclair and approved by the Native nations. Soon after this ceremony, Brisbois relocated to Prairie du Chien. In 1820, Brisbois' testimony to Isaac Lee helped many of the residents of the prairie gain title to the land on which they lived and farmed.

Brisbois continued in the fur trade, then in the early 19th century he changed his occupation. While living at Mackinac, he married Domitille Gauthier. When they relocated to Prairie du Chien, Michel purchased a lot and house in the Main Village from Louis Honoré. He had previously acquired several farms lots on which, like his neighbors, he grew rye and barley.[357] Brisbois built several ovens and established himself as a baker, hiring Strange Powers. He baked bread for the residents of the prairie and large quantities of hard biscuits for fur companies. Biscuits and corn or yellow pea soup were the staples of voyageurs as they paddled the large canoes on the Mississippi River, the Fox-Wisconsin waterway, and the Great Lakes.

Domitille Gauthier Brisbois

Born – 1781, Michilimackinac
Baptized – 15 July 1786, Michilimackinac[358]
Married – 6 August 1796, Michel Brisbois, at Michilimackinac[359]
Died – November 1846, at Prairie du Chien[360]

Domitille Gauthier was the daughter of Charles Gauthier and Magdelaine Paschal Chevalier.[361] Michel and Domitille had nine children: Sophie, born 1797; Charles, born 1798; Joseph, born circa 1800; Louis Gabriel, born circa 1805; Marie Bernard Walter, born 1808; George Pascal, born 1810; Marie Louise, born 1814; Marguerite Domitille, born 1816; and Caritime, born 1818.

Marie Bernard Walter Brisbois

Born – 4 October 1808[362]
Baptized – 29 April 1817, at Prairie du Chien[363]
Married – 10 September 1832 Therese LaChapelle, at Prairie du Chien[364]
Died – 15 June 1885, at Mendota, Wisconsin.

Bernard Brisbois was the son of Michel and Domitille Brisbois. As a young man, he worked for the American Fur Company, but as the fur trade declined, he went into business for a short time with Henry M. Rice. Their partnership ended, and in 1850-1851 Brisbois, known as B. W., had a stone store constructed north of his home in the old Main Village of Prairie du Chien. He operated a general dry goods store.

Bernard and his family lived in the stone house built in 1837 for Jane Fisher Rolette. The house was part of the separation agreement between Jane and Joseph Rolette. (See Joseph Rolette.) When the separation occurred, Bernard, Jane's cousin, had been appointed her legal representative. When Jane married Hercules L. Dousman in 1844, she gave the stone house to Bernard.

Bernard was appointed U.S. Postmaster in 1857, elected Crawford County sheriff, and held the office of county treasurer. In 1872, President Ulysses S. Grant appointed Brisbois a consul to Vernier, Belgium. Ill health forced Brisbois to resign and return to Prairie du Chien. He died while visiting his brother, who resided at Mendota, Wisconsin.[365]

Therese LaChapelle Brisbois

Born – 27 April 1815[366]
Married – 10 September 1832, at Prairie du Chien[367]
Died – 23 July 1849, at Prairie du Chien[368]

Therese Lachapelle was the daughter of Antoine and Pelagie Lapointe Lachapelle. In 1825, Antoine Lachapelle was living in the Township of Williamsburg, Illinois; but by 1830, he and his family were residing at Prairie du Chien.[369]

Bernard and Therese had five children: Josephine Sophie, born 29 August 1833; William, born February 1838, Daniel, born 11 March 1841; Emily, born 20 January 1843, and Henry, born 1845

Therese had been ill for three years before her death. She was "for several years a consistent member of the Presbyterian church in this village [Prairie du Chien], and by her Christian deportment, intelligence, and amiability had won esteem and lasting friendship of all her acquaintances. At home, she exhibited all the virtues that adorn the character of woman and heighten the pleasures of the fireside."[370]

Joseph A. Tilmont

Born – 25 May 1818, Brussels, Belgium[371]
Died – 25 February 1879, Prairie du Chien[372]

Joseph Tilmont was born in Belgium and in 1856 immigrated to the United States. In 1857, he settled at Prairie du Chien. He had been an officer in the Dutch army and had been stationed in India, where he served ten years. Joseph Tilmont married Stephanie Roze in 1849, and his household in 1860 included Stephain, age twenty-eight, and Alexander, age ten. Both individuals had been born in Belgium. In the 1870 census, both Tilmont and his son Alexander listed their occupations as "Druggist."[373]

People who died at Prairie du Chien, prior to May 10, 1817. Place of Burial Unknown, Alphabetical

Michel Pelletier *dit* Antaya

Baptized – 7 March 1749, Sorel, Canada

Married – 30 April 1778 Marie Menard, at St. Louis

Died – between 7 May 1804 and 2 May 1807

Many French had *dit* last names. A *dit* name is essentially an alias, or alternate name, tacked on to a family name or surname. *Dit* is a French form of the word *dire*, which means "to say," and in the case of *dit* names is translated loosely as "that is to say," or "called." Therefore, the family's original surname is the one passed down to them by an ancestor, while the "dit" name is the name the person/family is actually "called" or known as.

Michel's family name was Pelletier, but he also had a *dit* name, which was Antaya. In the records pertaining to Michel's residence at Prairie du Chien, his name was recorded as Antaya.

Michel Antaya was the son of Jacques Pelletier *dit* Antaya and Marguerite Abraham *dit* Desmarais. Michel removed to Kaskaskia to engage in the fur trade. He married Marie Menard, the daughter of Paul Menard and Jeannete Lamere at St. Louis on April 30, 1778. Michel and

Marie had several daughters: Marie, baptized at Vincennes, Indiana on January 1779; Marguerite, baptized at St. Louis on May 4, 1781; and Marie Angelique, baptized at St. Genevieve, Missouri on June 1, 1784.[374] After the birth of their third daughter, the family moved to Prairie du Chien.

Michel Antaya and his wife Marie Menard sold a house and lot in Prairie du Chien to Jean Baptiste Bertholet on May 7, 1804. On May 2, 1807, Marie Menard, "widow of Michel Peltier *dit* Antaya," sold a tract of land in the Illinois County. Michel Pelletier *dit* Antaya died sometime between the two sales. In 1807, Marie still resided at Prairie du Chien.[375]

Pierre Pelletier *dit* Antaya

Baptized – 19 February 1746 at St-François-du-Lac, Yamaska, Canada
Married – Kee-Zish (le Soleil/The Sun)
Died – prior to 3 May 1805

Michel Pelletier *dit* Antaya and Pierre Antaya were brothers. In 1763, Pierre Antaya signed an engagement at Montreal with Nicolas Marchessau to go to "la Baye." He continued in the fur trade and by the summer of 1779, Antaya was one of the proprietors of the General Store at Michilimackinac. The Store was owned by an association of traders who operated from Michilimackinac. Antaya had one canoe of merchandise at Prairie du Chien. He traveled between Michilimackinac, Prairie du Chien, and St. Louis, finally settling at the prairie by 1783.

Antaya witnessed the agreement between Julien Dubuque and the Meskwaki dated September 22, 1788, in which the Meskwaki allowed Dubuque to mine lead on their lands.

Pierre Antaya and Kee-Zish (baptized as Catherine May 6, 1817, at Prairie du Chien by Father Dunand) had eleven children: Elizabeth, born circa 1783 (see Elizabeth Antaya Cardinal, Oulette); Marguerite, born circa 1785; Pierre, born circa 1786; Josette, born circa 1787; Marie, born circa 1790; Theodiste, born circa 1795; Euphrosine, born circa 1796 (see Strange Powers); Catherine, born circa 1797; and Isadore, born circa 1798.[376]

Antaya acquired several village and farm lots at Prairie du Chien. He lived on Main Village Lot No. 11. After selling the lot to Augustin Roc,

Pierre and his family lived in a large house built at the west end of Farm Lot No. 15.[377]

When Michel Labathe died (prior to May 3, 1805), a list of debts owed by the Labathe estate had been compiled. Included in the list of debts was money owed to Pierre Antaya. The list was dated May 3, 1805. Antaya was listed as "Pierre Antaya dec'd."[378]

Claude Gagnier

Died – 1803

Claude Gagnier was of French-Canadian ancestry. By 1778, he owned land and farmed at Cahokia, a French settlement founded by missionaries from Quebec, located across the Mississippi River from St. Louis. He had also worked a number of trading seasons for Michel Brisbois, who lived at Prairie du Chien. Brisbois traded with the Ho-Chunk, and Gagnier transported pelts to Chicago that Brisbois had acquired in those trades. Gagnier, in traveling between the three communities, would have been familiar with Prairie du Chien.[379]

In 1792, Claude Gagnier paddled up the Mississippi River to Prairie du Chien seeking a lot on which to make a home for his family. He had formed a marital union with Marianne Labuche. He selected an unsettled tract located at the far north end of the prairie, which came to be known as Farm Lot No. 2. Two years later, he selected a very large strip of the prairie a half mile south of Farm Lot No. 2. Gagnier partitioned that property and sold the northern portion to Pierre LeFleur.[380]

Claude Gagnier cultivated and then occupied the southern portion of the tract, and it came to be called Farm Lot No. 13. Gagnier built a sizeable house for Marianne and what would become their large family. The house was west of the dirt road "highway" that traversed the prairie. By 1794, Marianne and her son from a previous union, François Duchouquette, joined him.

No record of a marriage between Claude Gagnier and Marianne Labuche has been found. In the few years they were together, they had six children born between 1795 and 1802. They named their sons François Regis (see Registre Gagnier), Claude (see Claude Gagnier), and Bazil. Their daughters were Helene, Adelaide, and Melanie. Adelaide and Melanie may have been twins, as they were both fifteen when they were baptized in 1817 by Father Dunand.[381]

Michel Labathe

Died – Before 7 May 1804

Little is known of Michel Labathe, but by 1786 he was at Michilimackinac. Labathe seems to have traded between Michilimackinac, Prairie du Chien, and the Illinois Country. When St. Clair County was organized as part of the Territory of Indiana in 1800, Michel was appointed an ensign in the 7th regiment of the county militia.

Labathe formed a marital relationship with Angelique, a daughter of the second Wapasha.[382] They had at least two children. Arcange was baptized on May 1, 1817, at the age of fourteen. François was baptized in St. Louis in 1815. An inventory of the estate of Michel Labathe, which he held at Prairie du Chien, was made by Michel Brisbois and Phillip La Saussey. It included an extensive inventory of trade goods and a well-furnished home.[383]

Baptiste Lapointe

Died – About 1807

Baptiste was the son of Charles Lapointe and Suzanne Antaya. He died at a young age.[384]

Felix Mercier

Died – Prior to 1812

Felix had been married to Marie Louise Giard. Marie Louise then married François Chenevert. On April 26, 1817, Father Dunand baptized Nicola, born April 29, 1812, and Bazil, born March 7, 1815. Both were the children of François Chenevert and Marie Louise Giard Mercier.[385]

Part One Endnotes

1 *American State Papers, Public Lands*, vol. 4, Documents, Legislative and Executive of the Congress of the United States, from the First Session of the Fourteenth to the First Session of the Eighteenth Congress, Inclusive, 34 vols., (Washington DC: Gales and Seaton, 1834), 854.

2 James H. Lockwood, "Early Times and Events in Wisconsin," *Collections of the State Historical Society of Wisconsin,* vol. 4, (Madison: Wisconsin Historical Society), 2:128.

3 James L. Hansen, "Prairie du Chien's Earliest Church Records, 1817," *Minnesota Genealogical Journal,* no. 4 (Nov 1985), 329-342.

4 James L. Hansen, "Prairie du Chien and Galena Church Records, 1827-1829," *Minnesota Genealogical Journal,* no. 5 (May 1986), 421-442.

5 *Register de Catholicité de la Praire du Chien 1840,* Archives Diocese of La Crosse, La Crosse, Wisconsin.

6 Strange Powers to Frederic Rese, Catholic Bishop of Detroit, 16 February 1836, *Deeds A,* Crawford County Register of Deeds, Prairie du Chien, Wisconsin.

7 Hercules L. to Frederic Rese, Catholic Bishop of Detroit, 13 February 1836, *Deeds A,* Crawford County Register of Deeds, Prairie du Chien, Wisconsin.

8 Notes of Florence Bittner written at Prairie du Chien. Owned by the author.

9 "A Scrap of History. Some Facts Relative to an Ancient Burial Ground," *Green Bay Weekly Gazette,* 23 October 1886.

10 Hamilton Nelson Ross, *Village Outpost on Madeline Island,* (Madison: State Historical Society of Wisconsin, 2000).

11 *American State Papers, Public Lands,* vol. 4, 851.

12 Paul M. Judson, "Sketch of the Life of Father Gabriel Richard 1767-1832," *Records of the American Catholic Historical Society of Philadelphia,* vol. 37, no. 3 (September 1926), 250-297.

13 "Bishop Flaget's Report of the Diocese of Bardstown to Pius VII, 10 April 1815," *The Catholic Historical Review,* vol. 1 (April 1915-January 1916), 310-319.

14 Francis Paul Prucha, ed., *Documents of United States Indian Policy,* (Lincoln: University of Nebraska Press, 1990), 28-29.

15 Lockwood, "Early Times and Events in Wisconsin," 98-196.

16 Ibid.

17 "Field Notes of the Surveys of Private Land Claims at Michilimackinac, Green Bay, and Prairie du Chien: Surveyed in 1828, by John Mullet & Lucius Lyon, Dep. Surveyors," Grand Rapids Public Library, Grand Rapids, Michigan.

18 "To the Congress of the United States of America..." (manuscript petition by the residents of Prairie du Chien, Wisconsin, 1816) online facsimile at www.wisconsinhistory.org/turningpoints/search.asp?id=1755. Visited on: 4/8/2022; Lockwood, "Early Times and Events in Wisconsin," 2:128.

19 Camillus Maes, *The Life of Charles Nerinckx,* (Robert Clarke & Co.: Cincinnati, 1880), 100-129.

20 Ella M. E. Flick, trans., "Diary of the Reverend Father Marie Joseph Dunand," *Records of the American Catholic Historical Society of Philadelphia,* vol. 27, 1916, 45-64.

21 Flick, "Diary of the Reverend Father Marie Joseph Dunand," 45-64.

22 Ibid.

23 Hansen, "Prairie du Chien's Earliest Church Records, 1817."

24 Flick, "Diary of the Reverend Father Marie Joseph Dunand," 45-64

25 Ibid.

26 Flick, "Diary of the Reverend Marie Joseph Dunand," 45-64; Hansen, "Prairie du Chien's Earliest Church Records, 1817," 329-342.

27 Hansen, "Prairie du Chien's Earliest Church Records, 1817," 329-342.

28 Ibid.

29 Flick, "Diary of the Reverend Marie Joseph Dunand," 45-64.

30 Flick, "Diary of the Reverend Marie Joseph Dunand," 45-64; Hansen, "Prairie du Chien's Earliest Church Records, 1817."

31 Ella M. E. Flick, trans., "Epistle or Diary of the Reverend Father Marie Joseph Dunand," *Records of the American Catholic Historical Society of Philadelphia,* vol. 26, 99-105; Ella M. E. Flick, trans., "Diary of the Reverend Father Marie Joseph Dunand," *Records of the American Catholic Historical Society of Philadelphia,* vol. 27, 1916, 45-64.

32 Hansen, "Prairie du Chien's Earliest Church Records, 1817," 329-342.

33 *1810 US Federal Census, Illinois Territory, St. Clair County, Prairie du Chien, 1820 US Federal Census, Michigan Territory, Crawford County, Prairie du Chien,* ancestry.com.

34 John F. Marszalek, "Who Was Stephen Badin?" *Notre Dame Magazine,* Summer 1994, magazine.nd.edu/stories.

35 Richard C. Elliot, "Sketch of the Life and Times of Rev. Gabriel Richard of Detroit Michigan," *The American Catholic Historical Researches,* October 1899, 155-176.

36 James L. Hansen, "Prairie du Chien and Galena Church Records, 1827-1829," *Minnesota Genealogical Journal,* no. 5, 421-442.

37 François Vincent Badin to Parish Priest of St. Louis, 9 June 1827 published in John Rothensteiner, "The Northeastern Part of the Diocese of St. Louis under Bishop Rosati," *Illinois Catholic Historical Review,* vol. 2 no. 2, 185.

38 James L. Hansen, "Crawford County Marriages, 1816-1848," *Minnesota Genealogical Journal* vol. 1, 3-56.

39 François Vincent Badin to Joseph Rosati, 30 August 1827 published in John Rothensteiner, "The Northeastern Part of the Diocese of St. Louis under Bishop Rosati," 187.

40 François Vincent Badin to Parish Priest of St. Louis, 9 June 1827 published in John Rothensteiner, "The Northeastern Part of the Diocese of St. Louis under Bishop Rosati," 185.

41 James L. Hansen, "Prairie du Chien and Galena Church Records, 1827-1829."

42 Ibid.

43 Ibid.

44 Ibid.

45 François Vincent Badin to Joseph Rosati, 30 August 1827 published in John Rothensteiner, "The Northeastern Part of the Diocese of St. Louis under Bishop Rosati," 186.

46 Ibid.

47 Ibid.

48 James L. Hansen, "Prairie du Chien and Galena Church Records, 1827-1829."

49 François Vincent Badin to Joseph Rosati, 30 August 1827, 186; James L. Hansen, "Prairie du Chien and Galena Church Records, 1827-1829."

50 James L. Hansen, "Prairie du Chien and Galena Church Records, 1827-1829."

51 "DuBourg and the Society of Jesus," 45-55, jesuitarchives.org.

52 John Rothensteiner, "The Northeastern Part of the Diocese of St. Louis under Bishop Rosati," 189-190.

53 Joseph Anthony Lutz to Bishop Rosati, 8 October 1830 published in John Rothensteiner, "The Northeastern Part of the Diocese of St. Louis under Bishop Rosati," 191-192.

54 Joseph Anthony Lutz to Bishop Rosati, 8 October 1830 published in John Rothensteiner, "The Northeastern Part of the Diocese of St. Louis under Bishop Rosati," 191.

55 John Rothensteiner, "The Northeastern Part of the Diocese of St. Louis under Bishop Rosati," 192-193.

56 *The Memoirs of Father Samuel Mazzuchelli, o.p.,* (Chicago: The Priory Press, 1967), 5.

57 Samuel Mazzuchelli to Bishop Joseph Rosati, 29 September 1832 in "The Northeastern Part of the Diocese of St. Louis under Bishop Rosati," 281-283.

58 *The Memoirs of Father Samuel Mazzuchelli,* 70-74.

59 Ibid, 124-125.

60 Peter L. Scanlan, *Centennial History of St. Gabriel's Parish, Prairie du Chien, Wisconsin,* (Prairie du Chien: Crawford County Press, 1936), 19.

61 *The Memoirs of Father Samuel Mazzuchelli,* 144-149.

62 Ibid, 161.

63 Peter L. Scanlan Papers, Area Research Center, University of Wisconsin-Platteville, Platteville, Wisconsin.

64 Strange Powers to Frederic Rese, 16 February 1836, *Deeds A,* Crawford County Register of Deeds, Prairie du Chien, Wisconsin; *The Memoirs of Father Samuel Mazzuchelli,* 161.

65 Samuel Mazzuchelli to Bishop Rosati, 14 July 1836, in John Rothensteiner, "The Northeastern Part of the Diocese of St. Louis under Bishop Rosati," *Illinois Catholic Historical Review,* vol. 3, no. 2, 130-131.

66 M. M. Hoffmann, *The Church Founders of the Northwest: Loras, Cretin and other Captains of Christ,* (Milwaukee: The Bruce Publishing Company, 1937), 129.

67 Transcription of records of the Dubuque Cathedral, Archives Diocese of La Crosse, La Crosse, Wisconsin.

68 "Account of Money received to Erect a Catholic church at Prairie du Chien," St. Gabriel's Church Archives, Prairie du Chien, Wisconsin.

69 *The Memoirs of Father Samuel Mazzuchelli,* 161.

70 *Register de Catholicité de la Praire du Chien 1840,* Archives Diocese of La Crosse, La Crosse, Wisconsin.

71 *Register de Catholicité de la Praire du Chien 1840* (copy), Peter L. Scanlan Papers, Mss D, Area Research Center, University of Wisconsin-Platteville,

72 *The Memoirs of Father Samuel Mazzuchelli,* 124-125.

73 Probate fille of Michel Brisbois, Crawford County Register in Probate, Prairie du Chien, Wisconsin.

74 *Deeds C,* Crawford County Register of Deeds, Prairie du Chien, Wisconsin.

75 *Deeds E,* Crawford County Register of Deeds, Prairie du Chien, Wisconsin.

76 *1 Certificate,* Crawford County Register of Deeds, Prairie du Chien, Wisconsin.

77 *The Courier,* 23 June 1885, Prairie du Chien, Wisconsin.

78 *1860 and 1870 U.S. Federal Census for Wisconsin, Crawford County, Prairie du Chien.*

Endnotes Part Two

1 James L. Hansen, "Prairie du Chien's Earliest Church Records, 1817," *Minnesota Genealogical Journal,* no. 4 (Nov 1985), 329-342.

2 Ibid.

3 "Amiot, Jean-Baptiste," *Dictionary of Canadian Biography,* biographie.ca.

4 Hansen, "Earliest Church Records," 329-342.

5 *Quebec, Canada Vital and Church Records (Drouin Collection)* 1621-1968, ancestry.com.

6 James L. Hansen, "Prairie du Chien and Galena Church Records, 1827-1829" in *Minnesota Genealogical Journal,* no. 5 (May 1986), 421-442.

7 Petition of half-breeds claim, William Clark Papers, microfilm reel MS-99, Kansas Historical Society, ksks.org.

8 *American State Papers, Public Lands, vol. 4, Documents, Legislative and Executive of the Congress of the United States, from the First Session of the Fourteenth to the First Session of the Eighteenth Congress, Inclusive,* 34 vols., (Washington DC: Gales and Seaton, 1834), 854.

9 William D. Pratt, *A History of the National Guard in Indiana* (Indianapolis: W. D. Pratt, 1909), accessed online at www.archive.org/details/historyofnationa00inprat, 13.

10 "To the Congress of the United States of America..." (manuscript petition by the residents of Prairie du Chien, Wisconsin, 1816) online facsimile at www.wisconsinhistory.org/turningpoints/search.asp?id=1755.

11 *Deeds B,* Crawford County Registers of Deeds, Prairie du Chien, Wisconsin.

12 Hansen, "Earliest Church Records," 329-342.

13 Ibid.

14 Ibid.

15 Ibid.

16 Ibid.

17 Ibid.

18 James L. Hansen, "The Pelletier *dit* Antaya Families of Prairie du Chien," *The Genealogist*, vol. 32, no.1, Spring 2018, 104-131.

19 Hansen, "Earliest Church Records," 329-342.

20 Ibid.

21 Donna Valley Russell, *Michigan Voyageurs from the Notary Book of Samuel Abbott, Mackinac Island 1807-1817,* (Detroit: Detroit Society for Genealogical Research, Inc. 1982), 33.

22 To the Congress of the United States of America..." (manuscript petition by the residents of Prairie du Chien, Wisconsin, 1816) online facsimile at www.wisconsinhistory.org/turningpoints/search.asp?id=1755.

22 Hansen, "Earliest Church Records," 392-342.

24 Ibid.

25 Ibid.

26 Ibid.

27 Ibid.

28 Hansen, "Galena," 421-442.

29 Hansen, "Earliest Church Records," 329-342.

30 Ibid.

31 "Reminiscence of Theresa Barrette," *History of Crawford and Richland Counties, Wisconsin,* (Springfield IL: Union Publishing Company, 1884), 563-564.

32 Hansen, "Earliest Church Records," 329-342.

33 *Deeds A,* Crawford County Register of Deeds, Prairie du Chien, Wisconsin.

34 Ibid.

35 Hansen, "Earliest Church Records," 329-342.

36 Voyageur Database, archivesshsb.mb.ca.

37 *1840 US Federal Census, Michigan Territory, Crawford County, 1850 US Federal Census, Wisconsin, Crawford County.*

38 Hansen, "Earliest Church Records," 329-342.

39 Ibid.

40 Probate file of Pierre Gosselin, Crawford County Register in Probate, Prairie du Chien, Wisconsin.

41 Donna Valley Russell, *Michigan Voyageurs from the Notary Book of Samuel Abbott, Mackinac Island 1807-1817,* (Detroit: Detroit Society for Genealogical Research, Inc. 1982), 19-36.

42 "List of Canadian Voyageurs who volunteered their services..." in *Wisconsin Historical Collections,* 9:262-264.

43 "Roster of American Fur Company Employees for the Years 1818-1819," *Wisconsin Historical Collections,* 12:160; William Clark Papers, Kansas Historical Society.

44 Probate file Pierre Gosselin, Crawford County Register in Probate, Prairie du Chien, Wisconsin.

45 Hansen, "Earliest Church Records," 329-342.

46 To the Congress of the United States of America..." (manuscript petition by the residents of Prairie du Chien, Wisconsin, 1816) online facsimile at www.wisconsinhistory.org/turningpoints/search.asp?id=1755.

47 *American State Papers, Public Lands, vol. 4,* 867-869.

48 B. W. Brisbois, "Traditions and Recollections of Prairie du Chien," *Wisconsin Historical Collections,* 9:282-302.

49 Hansen, "Earliest Church Records," 329-342.

50 *American State Papers, Public Lands, vol. 4,* 871.

51 Hansen, "Earliest Church Records," 329-342.

52 James L. Hansen, "Crawford County Marriages, 1816-1848," *Minnesota Genealogical Journal* 1 (1984), 39–58.

53 Hansen, "Marriages," 39-58.

54 Probate file Victoire Findley, Crawford County Register in Probate, Prairie du Chien, Wisconsin.

55 James H. Lockwood, "Early Times and Events in Wisconsin" in *Wisconsin Historical Collections*, 2:149-150.

56 James H. Lockwood, "Early Times at Prairie du Chien" in *Wisconsin Historical Collections,* 2:127.

57 Hansen, "Earliest Church Records," 329-342.

58 Hansen, "Marriages," 39-58.

59 Voyageur Database, archivesshsb.mb.ca.

60 Hansen, "Earliest Church Records," 329-342.

61 Hansen, "Marriages," 39-58.

62 *Deeds A,* Crawford County Register of Deeds, Prairie du Chien, Wisconsin.

63 Hansen, "Earliest Church Records," 329-342.

64 James L. Hansen, "The Rolette Family of Prairie du Chien," manuscript.

65 Hansen, "Rolette" manuscript.

66 Hansen, "Galena," 421-442.

67 Hansen, "Earliest Church Records," 329-342.

68 Hansen, "Marriages," 39-58.

69 Hansen, "Galena," 421-442.

70 Hansen, "Earliest Church Records," 329-342.

71 Hansen, "Galena," 421-442.

72 Ibid.

73 Ibid.

74 Ibid.

75 Hansen, "Earliest Church Records," 329-342

76 Hansen, "Galena," 421-442.

77 Hansen, "Earliest Church Records," 329-342.

78 *American State Papers, Public Lands, vol. 4*, 867-879.

79 Probate file of Denis Courtois, Crawford County Register in Probate, Prairie du Chien, Wisconsin.

80 Hansen, "Galena," 421-442.

81 Ibid.

82 Probate file of Jean Baptiste Wemette, Crawford County Register in Probate, Prairie du Chien, Wisconsin.

83 Ibid.

84 Hansen, "Galena," 421-442.

85 Ibid.

86 Ibid.

87 Petition of half-breeds claim, William Clark Papers, microfilm reel MS-99, Kansas Historical Society, ksks.org.

88 Hansen, "Earliest Church Records," 329-342.

89 Hansen, "Galena," 421-442.

90 Ibid.

91 Voyageur Database, archivesshsb.mb.ca.

92 *American State Papers, Public Lands, vol. 4*, 867-879.

93 "To the Congress of the United States of America..." (manuscript petition by the residents of Prairie du Chien, Wisconsin, 1816) online facsimile at www.wisconsinhistory.org/turningpoints/search.asp?id=1755.

94 "Roster of American Fur Company Employees for the Years 1818-1819" in *Wisconsin Historical Collections*; 12:160.

95 Hansen, "Earliest Church Records," 329-342.

96 Probate file Augustin Hebert, Crawford County Register in Probate, Prairie du Chien, Wisconsin

97 Hansen, "Galena," 421-442.

98 Ibid.

99 Hansen, "Marriages," 39-58.

100 Hansen, "Earliest Church Records," 329-342.

101 Hansen, "Earliest Church Records," 329-342.

102 Hansen, "Galena," 421-442.

103 Donna Valley Russell, *Michigan Voyageurs from the Notary Book of Samuel Abbott, Mackinac Island 1807-1817,* (Detroit: Detroit Society for Genealogical Research, Inc: 1982), 7, 17, 23, 26.

104 *American State Papers, Public Lands, vol. 4*, 867-879.

105 "Roster of American Fur Company Employees for the Years 1818-1819," *Wisconsin Historical Collections*, 12:160.

106 Probate file of Benjamin Cadotte, Crawford County Register in Probate, Prairie du Chien, Wisconsin.

107 Hansen, "Earliest Church Records," 329-342.

108 Hansen, "Marriages," 39-58.

109 Hansen, "Galena," 421-442.

110 Ibid.

111 Ibid.

112 Ibid.

113 Ibid.

114 Ibid.

115 Hansen, "Earliest Church Records," 329-342.

116 Hansen, "Marriages," 39-58.

117 *Baptisms, Marriages and Burials*, St. Gabriel's Parish, Archives of the Diocese of La Crosse, La Crosse, Wisconsin.

118 Hansen, "Marriages," 39-58..

119 Hansen, "Earliest Church Records," 329-342.

120 *Deeds C*, Crawford County Register of Deeds, Prairie du Chien, Wisconsin.

121 List of Canadian Voyageurs who volunteered their services...," *Wisconsin Historical Collections*, 9:262-264.

122 Joseph Tassé, *Les Canadiennes de l'Ouest*, (Montreal: d'Emprimerie Canadienne, 1878), 211; Calendar of the American Fur Company Papers.

123 St. Gabriel Church Records, Prairie du Chien, Diocese of La Crosse Archives, La Crosse, Wisconsin.

124 Joseph Tassé, *Les Canadiens de l'Ouest*, vol. 1, (Montreal: d'Emprimerie Canadienne, 1878), 145.

125 James L. Hansen, "Crawford County Marriages, 1816-1848," *Minnesota Genealogical Journal* 1 (1984), 39–58.

126 Hansen, "Marriages," 39-58.

127 Joseph Tassé, *Les canadiens de l'Ouest*, vol 1, (Montreal: d'Emprimerie Canadienne, 1878), 145-147.

128 *Deeds A*, Crawford County Register of Deeds, Prairie du Chien, Wisconsin.

129 Hansen, "Earliest Church Records," 329-342.

130 Hansen, "Marriages," 39-58.

131 *Deeds A*, Crawford County Register of Deeds, Prairie du Chien, Wisconsin.

132 Hansen, "Marriages," 39-58.

133 *Deeds A*, Crawford County Register of Deeds, Prairie du Chien, Wisconsin.

134 James Lockwood, "Early Times and Events in Wisconsin," *Wisconsin Historical Collections,* vol. 4 (Madison: Wisconsin Historical Society, 1903), 2:128.

135 Indented Articles of Separation between Joseph Rolette and his wife Jane, 22 September 1836, copy in Hercules L. Dousman Family Papers, Wisconsin Historical Society.

136 Will of Joseph Rolette, Crawford County Register in Probate, Prairie du Chien, Wisconsin.

137 3 Wis. 466 (Wis. 1854) DOUSMAN and wife v. HOOE, Executrix, etc, Supreme Court of Wisconsin, June 1854, case-law.vlex.com.

138 Hansen, "Earliest Church Records," 329-342.

139 Ibid.

140 *Baptisms, Marriages and Burials*, St. Gabriel's Parish, Archives of the Diocese of La Crosse, La Crosse, Wisconsin.

141 Ibid.

142 Hansen, "Earliest Church Records," 329-342.

143 Will of Joseph Rolette, *Probate Book B,* Crawford County Register in Probate, Prairie du Chien, Wisconsin.

144 Will of Elizabeth Rolette, *Probate Book B,* Crawford County Register in Probate, Prairie du Chien, Wisconsin.

145 *Baptisms, Marriages and Burials*, St. Gabriel's Parish, Archives of the Diocese of La Crosse, La Crosse, Wisconsin.

146 Hansen, "Marriages," 39-58.

147 Ibid.

148 Probate file of Benjamin Cadotte, Crawford County Register in Probate, Prairie du Chien, Wisconsin.

149 Hansen, "Marriages," 39-58.

150 Hansen, "Pelletier *dit* Antaya Families," vol. 32, no. 1, Spring 2018, 104-131.

151 Hansen, "Earliest Church Records," 329-342.

152 Hansen, "Pelletier *dit* Antaya Families," vol. 32, no. 1, Spring 2018, 104-131.

153 Hansen, "Earliest Church Records," 329-342.

154 Hansen, "Pelletier *dit* Antaya Families," vol. 31, no. 2, Fall 2017, 191-217.

155 Hansen, "Pelletier *dit* Antaya Families," vol. 32, no. 1, Spring 2018, 104-131.

156 Hansen, "Earliest Church Records," 329-342.

157 Ibid.

158 Hansen, "Galena," 421-442.

159 Hansen, "Pelletier *dit* Antaya Families," vol. 32, no. 1, Spring 2018, 104-131.

160 Probate file Andre Bazin, Crawford County Register in Probate, Prairie du Chien, Wisconsin.

161 Hansen, "Earliest Church Records," 329-342.

162 Donna Valley Russell, *Michigan Voyageurs from the Notary Book of Samuel Abbott, Mackinac Island 1807-1817,* (Detroit: Detroit Society for Genealogical Research, Inc. 1982), 28.

163 *American State Papers, Public Lands, vol. 4,* 870.

164 "Muster Roll of Captain Thomas McNair's Company of the Michigan Militia, ordered into Service by His Excellency Lewis Case Governor of the Michigan Territory on the 4th Day of July 1827," content.wisconsinhistory.org.

165 Probate file Andre Bazin, Crawford County Register in Probate, Prairie du Chien, Wisconsin.

166 Records of St. Gabriel's Catholic Church, Prairie du Chien, at La Crosse Diocese Archives, La Crosse, Wisconsin.

167 Hansen, "Earliest Church Records," 329-342.

168 Hansen, "Galena," 421-442.

169 Hansen, "Earliest Church Records," 329-342.

170 Hansen, "Marriages," 39-58.

171 Hansen, "Pelletier *dit* Antaya Families," vol. 32, no. 1, Spring 2018, 104-131.

172 Voyageur Database, archivesshsb.mb.ca.

173 *American State Papers, Public Lands, vol. 4,* 5:310.

174 Hansen, "Pelletier *dit* Antaya Families," vol. 32, no. 1, Spring 2018, 104-131.

175 Ibid.

176 Hansen, "Earliest Church Records," 329-342.

177 Hansen, "Pelletier *dit* Antaya Families," vol. 32, no. 1, Spring 2018, 104-131.

178 Hansen, "Pelletier *dit* Antaya Families," vol. 32, no. 1, Spring 2018, 104-131.

179 Hansen, "Earliest Church Records," 329-342.

180 Hansen, "Marriages," 39-58.

181 Hansen, "Earliest Church Records," 329-342.

182 "The Winnebago War," *History of Crawford and Richland Counties,* (Chicago, Union Publishing Company, 1884).

183 Hansen, "Marriages," 39-58.

184 Joseph Tassé, *Les canadiens de l'Ouest,* vol, 1, (Montreal: d'Emprimerie Canadienne, 1878), 147.

185 Ibid.

186 Hansen, "Earliest Church Records," 329-342.

187 Joseph Tassé, *Les canadiens de l'Ouest,* vol I, (Montreal: d'Emprimerie Canadienne, 1878), 163.

188 Hansen, "Earliest Church Records," 329-342.

189 Probate file of Claude Gagnier, Crawford County Register in Probate, Prairie du Chien, Wisconsin.

190 Hansen, "Earliest Church Records," 329-342.

191 Probate file of Claude Gagnier, Crawford County Register in Probate, Prairie du Chien, Wisconsin.

192 Hansen, "Earliest Church Records," 329-342.

193 Ibid.

194 Probate file Magdelaine Gauthier, Crawford County Register in Probate, Prairie du Chien, Wisconsin.

195 Ibid.

196 Hansen, "Marriages," 39-58.

197 Hansen, "Earliest Church Records," 329-342.

198 Ibid.

199 Hansen, "Marriages," 39-58.

200 Dussaume et al. v. Burnett et al., District Court Records, Dubuque, Iowa.

201 Hansen, "Earliest Church Records," 329-342.

202 Probate file of Prudent Langlois, Crawford County Register in Probate, Prairie du Chien, Wisconsin.

203 Voyageur Database, archivesshsb.mb.ca.

204 "List of Canadian Voyageurs who volunteered their services...," *Wisconsin Historical Collections,* 9:262-264.

205 Probate file of Prudent Langlois, Crawford County Register in Probate, Prairie du Chien, Wisconsin.

206 Hansen, "Earliest Church Records," 329-342.

207 Hansen, "Marriages," 39-58.

208 Hansen, "Pelletier *dit* Antaya Families," vol. 32, no. 1, Spring 2018, 104-131.

209 Hansen, "Earliest Church Records," 329-342.

210 Probate file of François Lapointe, Crawford County Register in Probate, Prairie du Chien, Wisconsin.

211 Hansen, "Earliest Church Records," 329-342.

212 Probate file of François Lapointe, Crawford County Register in Probate, Prairie du Chien, Wisconsin.

213 Ibid.

214 Ibid.

215 Hansen, "Earliest Church Records," 329-342.

216 Hansen, "Marriages," 39-58.

217 Probate file Joachim Lapointe, Crawford County Register in Probate, Prairie du Chien, Wisconsin.

218 Hansen, "Earliest Church Records," 329-342.

219 Probate file of François Lapointe, Crawford County Register in Probate, Prairie du Chien, Wisconsin.

220 Probate file Joachim Lapointe, Crawford County Register in Probate, Prairie du Chien, Wisconsin.

221 *American State Papers, Public Lands,* 4:863-879.

222 Sophie Eddy to George Westervelt, no date in probate file of François Lapointe, Crawford County Register in Probate, Prairie du Chien, Wisconsin.

223 "Reminiscence of Theresa Barrette," *History of Crawford and Richland Counties,* (Springfield, Ill: Union Publishing Company, 1884), 564-566.

224 *American State Papers, Public Lands,* 4:863-879.

225 Sophie Eddy to George Westervelt, no date in probate file of François Lapointe, Crawford County Register in Probate, Prairie du Chien, Wisconsin.

226 Sophie Eddy to George Westervelt, no date in probate file of François Lapointe, Crawford County Register in Probate, Prairie du Chien, Wisconsin.

227 Hansen, "Earliest Church Records," 329-342.

228 James L. Hansen, "Crawford County Marriages, 1816-1848," *Minnesota Genealogical Journal* 1 (1984), 39–58.

229 Ibid.

230 Hansen, "Pelletier *dit* Antaya Families," vol. 32, no. 1, Spring 2018, 104-131.

231 Probate file of Joseph Lessard, Crawford County Register in Probate, Prairie du Chien, Wisconsin.

232 Hansen, "Earliest Church Records," 329-342.

233 Hansen, "Marriages," 39-58.

234 Hansen, "Galena," 421-442.

235 Probate file Michel Lariviere, Crawford County Register in Probate, Prairie du Chien, Wisconsin.

236 Hansen, "Earliest Church Records," 329-342.

237 Probate file of Michel Lariviere, Crawford County Register in Probate, Prairie du Chien, Wisconsin.

238 Probate file of Joseph Lessard, Crawford County Register in Probate, Prairie du Chien, Wisconsin.

239 Ibid.

240 Hansen, "Pelletier *dit* Antaya Families," vol. 32, no. 1, Spring 2018, 104-131.

241 Hansen, "Earliest Church Records," 329-342.

242 Hansen, "Marriages," 39-58.

243 Probate file of Pierre Lessard, Crawford County Register in Probate, Prairie du Chien, Wisconsin.

244 Ibid.

245 Ibid.

246 Quebec, Canada, Vital and Church Records (Drouin Collection), 1621-1968, ancestry.com.

247 Hansen, "Earliest Church Records," 329-342.

248 Ibid.

249 Voyageur Database, archivesshsb.mb.ca.

250 "The Wisconsin Winnebagoes: an Interview with Moses Paquette," *Wisconsin Historical Collections* 12:399-433.

251 "The Wisconsin Winnebagoes: an Interview with Moses Paquette," *Wisconsin Historical Collections* 12:399-433.

252 Hansen, "Marriages," 39-58.

253 Probate file of Hardin Perkins, Crawford County Register in Probate, Prairie du Chien, Wisconsin.

254 Hansen, "Galena," 421-442.

255 Probate file of Hardin Perkins, Crawford County Register in Probate, Prairie du Chien, Wisconsin.

256 Hansen, "Galena," 421-442.

257 Ibid.

258 Clayton County Register of Deeds, Elkader, Iowa.

259 "Baptismal Record of Christ Church Anglican at William Henry" (formerly Sorel), ancestry.com.

260 Hansen, "Marriages," 39-58.

261 Ibid.

262 *American State Papers, Public Lands, vol. 4*, 871-878; "Muster Roll Capt. Thomas McNair's Company of Michigan Militia, 4 July 1828," content.wisconsinhistory.org.

263 *Deeds A*, Crawford County Register of Deeds, Prairie du Chien, Wisconsin.

264 Probate file of Strange Powers, Crawford County Register in Probate, Prairie du Chien, Wisconsin.

265 James L. Hansen, "The Pelletier *dit* Antaya Families of Prairie du Chien," *The Genealogist*

266 Notes written by Florence Bittner of Prairie du Chien. Owned by the author.

267 Probate file Akane [Etienne] Precour, Crawford County Register in Probate, Prairie du Chien, Wisconsin.

268 Hansen, "Earliest Church Records," 329-342.

269 Donna Valley Russell, *Michigan Voyageurs from the Notary Book of Samuel Abbott, Mackinac Island 1807-1817,* (Detroit: Detroit Society for Genealogical Research, Inc. 1982), 14.

270 Hansen, "Earliest Church Records," 329-342.

271 Ibid.

272 Probate file Provost François, Crawford County Register in Probate, Prairie du Chien, Wisconsin.

273 Hansen, "Earliest Church Records," 329-342.

274 Ibid.

275 Ibid.

276 Hansen, "Galena," 421-442.

277 Ibid.

278 Ibid.

279 Hansen, "Marriages," 39-58.

280 Ibid.

281 Hansen, "Galena," 421-442.

282 Probate file of Jean Marie Queré, Crawford County Register in Probate, Prairie du Chien, Wisconsin.

283 *American State Papers, Public Lands, vol. 4,* 871.

284 Winfield T. Durbin, *A History of the National Guard in Indiana,* (Indianapolis: W. D. Pratt, 1901), 15.

285 Probate file of Jean Marie Queré, Crawford County Register in Probate, Prairie du Chien, Wisconsin.

286 Hansen, "Marriages," 39-58.

287 Hansen, "Galena," 421-442.

288 Ibid.

289 Hansen, "Earliest Church Records," 329-342.

290 Ibid.

291 Hansen, “Marriages,” 39-58.

292 *Baptisms, Marriages and Burials*, St. Gabriel’s Parish, Archives of the Diocese of La Crosse, La Crosse, Wisconsin.

293 “St-Antoine-de-Rivière-du-Loup,” *Quebec, Canada, Vital and Church Records, 1621-1968,* ancestry.com.

294 Hansen, “Earliest Church Records,” 329-342.

295 Hansen, “Marriages,” 39-58.

296 “St-Antoine-de-Rivière-du-Loup” in *Quebec, Canada, Vital and Church Records, 1621-1968,* ancestry.com.

297 Voyageur Database, archivesshsb.mb.ca.

298 Mary Antoine de Julio, “The Vertefeuille House of Prairie du Chien: A Survivor from the Era of French Wisconsin,” *Wisconsin Magazine of History*, vol. 80, no. 1, Autumn 1996, 36-56.

299 Hansen, “Galena,” 421-442.

300 Hansen, “Marriages,” 39-58.

301 Probate file of Jean Baptiste Wemette, Crawford County Register in Probate, Prairie du Chien, Wisconsin.

302 Contract of marriage between Jean Baptiste Ouellette and Elizabeth Antailla in Crawford County Clerk Marriage Certificate, Prairie du Chien, Wisconsin.

303 Probate file of Jean Baptiste Wemette, Crawford County Register in Probate, Prairie du Chien, Wisconsin.

304 Ibid.

305 Grave marker, St. Gabriel’s Cemetery, Prairie du Chien, Wisconsin.

306 1850 *US Federal Census, Wisconsin, Crawford County, Prairie du Chien,*ancestry.com.

307 *Quebec, Canada, Vital and Church Records (Drouin Collection, 1621-1968*, ancestry.com.

308 Find A Grave.com.

309 Hansen, "Earliest Church Records," 329-342.

310 *Baptisms, Marriages and Burials*, St. Gabriel's Parish, Archives of the Diocese of La Crosse, La Crosse, Wisconsin.

311 Grave markers, St. Gabriel's Cemetery.

312 *Quebec, Canada Vital and Church Records (Drouin Collection), 1621-1968,* ancestry.com.

313 Hansen, "Galena," 421-442.

314 *Baptisms, Marriages and Burials*, St. Gabriel's Parish, Archives of the Diocese of La Crosse, La Crosse, Wisconsin.

315 *1850 US Federal Census, Wisconsin, Crawford County, Prairie du Chien,* ancestry.com.

316 *Baptisms, Marriages and Burials*, St. Gabriel's Parish, Archives of the Diocese of La Crosse, La Crosse, Wisconsin.

376 Image of entry from a bible posted by Charles McCoy on ancestry.com.

318 *U. S. Army, Register of Enlistments, 1798-1914;* (National Archives Microfilm Publication M233, 81 rolls) Records Group 94, National Archives.

319 Hansen, "Marriages," 39-58.

320 "Recollections of Antoine Grignon," *Proceedings of the State Historical Society of Wisconsin at its annual meeting held October 22 and December 19, 1913.*

321 *Baptisms, Marriages and Burials*, St. Gabriel's Parish, Archives of the Diocese of La Crosse, La Crosse, Wisconsin.

322 "American Fur Company Invoices, 1821-1822" in *Wisconsin Historical Collections,* 11:370-379.

323 *Genealogical Dictionary of Canadian Families* (Tanguay Collection), 1608-1890, vol. 7, Sect.1, page 50, ancestry.com.

324 Hansen, "Marriages," 39-58.

325 *Baptisms, Marriages and Burials*, St. Gabriel's Parish, Archives of the Diocese of La Crosse, La Crosse, Wisconsin.

326 "The history of Fort Winnebago as narrated by Hon. Sat. Clark at the courthouse in Portage, on Friday Eve., Mar. 21, '79," *Wisconsin Local History and Biography Articles,* wisconsinhistory.org.

327 Pierre Paquette, "Wisconsin Historical Dictionary," wisconsinhistory.org.

328 "Narrative of John T. De La Ronde," *Wisconsin Historical Collections*, 7:356-359; "The history of Fort Winnebago as narrated by Hon. Sat. Clark at the court house in Portage, on Friday Eve., Mar. 21, '79," *Wisconsin Local History and Biography Articles,* wisconsinhistory.org.

329 James L. Hansen, "The Campbell Family of Prairie du Chien," manuscript, 1999.

330 Hansen, "Marriages," 39-58.

331 Hansen, "Galena," 421-442.

332 Donna Valley Russell, *Michigan Voyageurs from the Notary Book of Samuel Abbott, Mackinac Island 1807-1817,* (Detroit: Detroit Society for Genealogical Research, Inc. 1982), 19. 24. 30.

333 Hansen, "Galena," 421-442.

334 *Wisconsin Historical Collections,* 20:314.

335 *Congressional Series of the United States, Public Documents,* vol. 219. "1825-1826 Trader Licenses," mainlymichigan.com; "*Licenses to trade with Indians,* Letter from the Secretary of War transmitting an abstract of licenses granted to trade with Indians within the year commencing 10th September, 1832," digitalcommons.law.ou.edu.

336 "Narrative of John T. De La Ronde," *Wisconsin Historical Collections*, 7:360; Probate file of Edward Pizanne, Crawford County Register in Probate, Prairie du Chien, Wisconsin.

337 Hansen, "Earliest Church Records," 329-342.

338 Rhoda Gilman, AIRD, JAMES in *Dictionary of Canadian Biography*, biographi.ca.

339 Rhoda Gilman, AIRD, JAMES in *Dictionary of Canadian Biography*, biographi.ca.

340 Ibid.

341 Probate file of James Aird, Crawford County Register in Probate, Prairie du Chien, Wisconsin.

342 Elizabeth Munro Fisher, *Memoirs of Mrs. Elizabeth Fisher of the City of New York*, (New York, 1810), 13.

343 Elizabeth Baird, "Reminiscences of Early Days on Mackinac Island," *Wisconsin Historical Collections*, vol. 14.

344 Fisher, "Memoirs," 13.

345 Mary Elise Antoine, *The War of 1812 in Wisconsin: the Battle for Prairie du Chien*, (Madison: Wisconsin Historical Society Press, 2016); 27, 28, 34, 36, 41, 43, 56, 90, 92, 126-7, 221, 228.

346 Elizabeth Baird, "Reminiscences of Early Days on Mackinac Island," *Wisconsin Historical Collections* vol. 14.

347 Probate file Henry M. Fisher, Crawford County Register in Probate, Prairie du Chien, Wisconsin.

348 U.S. *Army Register of Enlistments, 1798-1914*, https://www.ancestry.com/search/collections/1198/.

349 Ibid.

350 James H. Lockwood, "Early Times and Events in Wisconsin," *Wisconsin Historical Collections*, 2:160.

351 Hansen, "Galena," 421-442.

352 *Mémoires de la Société Généalogique Canadienne-Française*, (Montreal: January 1957), 169.

353 *"Neither White men nor Indians": Affidavits from the Winnebago Mixed-Blood Claims Commissions, 1838-1839*, (Roseville MN: Park Genealogical Books, 2002), 43.

354 "Mackinac Register of Marriages, 1725-1821," *Wisconsin Historical Collections*, vol. 18 (Madison: Wisconsin Historical Society, 1908), 469-514.

355 Probate file Michel Brisbois, Crawford County Register in Probate, Prairie du Chien, Wisconsin.

356 *Mémoires de la Société Généalogique Canadienne-Française*, (Montreal: January 1957), 169.

357 *American State Papers, Public Lands, vol. 4*, 863-870.

358 "Mackinac Baptisms," *Wisconsin Historical Collections*, 19:79.

359 "Mackinac Marriages," *Wisconsin Historical Collections*, 18:499.

360 Probate file Domitille Brisbois, Crawford County Register in Probate, Prairie du Chien, Wisconsin.

361 "Mackinac Baptisms," *Wisconsin Historical Collections*, 19:79.

362 Hansen, "Earliest Church Records," 329-342.

363 Ibid.

364 Hansen, "Marriages," 39-58.

365 W.H.C. Folsom, *Fifty Years in the Northwest*, (1888), 23-24.

366 Inscription on burial monument, Brisbois Cemetery, Prairie du Chien, Wisconsin.

367 Hansen, "Marriages," 39-58.

368 Inscription on burial monument, Brisbois Cemetery, Prairie du Chien, Wisconsin.

369 *Illinois State Census Collection, 1825*-1865; 1830 *U.S. Federal Census, Michigan Territory, Crawford County.*

370 *The Patriot*, July 1849, Prairie du Chien, Wisconsin.

371 Inscription on burial monument, Brisbois Cemetery, Prairie du Chien, Wisconsin.

372 *History of Crawford and Richland Counties*, (Springfield, IL: Union Publishing Company, 1884), 685.

373 *1860 and 1870 U.S. Federal Census for Wisconsin, Crawford County, Prairie du Chien.*

374 Hansen, "Pelletier *dit* Antaya Families," Fall 2017, 191-217.

375 Cahokia Book of Records, B:254, microfilm Illinois State Archives, Springfield, Illinois.

376 Hansen, "Pelletier *dit* Antaya Families," Fall 2017, 191-217.

377 *American State Papers, Public Lands, vol.* 4, 863-879.

378 Probate file of Michel la Bathe, Illinois State Archives, Springfield, Illinois.

379 *Cahokia records, 1778-1790.* (Springfield, Ill: Trustees of the Illinois State Library, 1907), 153.

380 Henri Duchouquette of Kaskaskia was known as Henri LaFleur. Claude may have had a connection of business or friendship to Pierre LaFleur, which again connects Marianne Labuche to this Duchouquette family from the Illinois Country. *American State Papers, Public Lands, vol. 4*, 867, 869.

381 Hansen, "Earliest Church Records," 329-342.

381 James Reed affidavit No. 89 "Testimony taken at Wabashaw, Wabashaw County, Minnesota Territory, August 20th to 25th inclusive, 1855 in behalf of certain 'Mixed Bloods,'" NARG 75, Bureau of Indian Affairs, Entry 529, Sioux Reserves.

382 Probate file of Michel la Bathe, Illinois State Archives, Springfield, Illinois.

383 Hansen, "Pelletier *dit* Antaya Families," vol. 32, no. 1, Spring 2018, 104-131.

384 Hansen, "Earliest Church Records," 329-342.

Index

C

D

E

F

G

H

I

M

Q

R

S

About the Author

Mary Elise Antoine was born and raised in Prairie du Chien. She graduated from Marquette University with a BA in History and holds a Masters' degree in History Museum Studies from New York State University–Oneonta. She resides in a restored French-Canadian house in Prairie du Chien.

Mary Elise has over 40 years professional experience working in historic preservation and for historic sites. While residing in New York State, she was Coordinator of Interpretation for the New York State Division of Historic Preservation and then was Director at Fort Johnson, the 1749 home of Sir William Johnson.

Returning to Prairie du Chien, for many years Mary Elise was Curator of Collections and Research at Villa Louis State Historic Site. She is on the Board and past-president of the Prairie du Chien Historical Society, where she coordinated the restoration of the St. Germain *dit* Gauthier House. She is the Wisconsin Ambassador for the French Heritage Corridor and on the board of the Wisconsin Trust for Historic Preservation.

Her published writings include: *The War of 1812 in Wisconsin: The Battle for Prairie du Chien; Frenchtown Chronicles of Prairie du Chien; Enslaved, Indenture, Free: Five Black Women in the Upper Mississippi* all published by Wisconsin Historical Society Press. *Images of Prairie du Chien, Legendary Locals of Prairie du Chien*—Arcadia Publishing. *Frenchtown Cemetery-Old Catholic Burying Ground Prairie du Chien, 1816-1840*—Little Creek Press.

Printed in the United States
by Baker & Taylor Publisher Services